BEST OF VENICE
YOUR #1 ITINERARY PLANNER FOR WHAT TO SEE, DO, AND EAT

Wanderlust Pocket Guides

Planning a trip to Italy?

Check out our other Wanderlust Pocket Travel Guides on Amazon:

BEST OF ITALY: YOUR #1 ITINERARY PLANNER FOR WHAT TO SEE, DO, AND EAT

BEST OF ROME: YOUR #1 ITINERARY PLANNER FOR WHAT TO SEE, DO, AND EAT

BEST OF FLORENCE AND TUSCANY: YOUR #1 ITINERARY PLANNER FOR WHAT TO SEE, DO, AND EAT

Also available:

BEST OF JAPAN: YOUR #1 ITINERARY PLANNER FOR WHAT TO SEE, DO, AND EAT

BEST OF TOKYO: YOUR #1 ITINERARY PLANNER FOR WHAT TO SEE, DO, AND EAT

BEST OF KYOTO: YOUR #1 ITINERARY PLANNER FOR WHAT TO SEE, DO, AND EAT

Our Free Gift to You

As purchasers of this paperback copy, we are offering you an **Amazon Matchbook download** of our colored **kindle version of this book for FREE.** Go to our book's page on Amazon and select the kindle version to download.

You **do not have to own a kindle** to read the kindle version of this book. Simply download the kindle reading app on your computer, tablet, or smartphone.

" A realist, in Venice, would become a romantic by mere faithfulness to what he saw before him. "

Arthur Symons

Table of Contents

REGIONS
OF ITALY

INTRODUCTION

The word "magical" comes up often when discussing Venice, this ancient and ethereal city built on the waters of the Venetian Lagoon. The city got its legendary beginning when ancient inhabitants of the region retreated to it as a marshy and defensible haven from invading barbarians. The network of canals, initially built as part of this defense system, has unexpectedly given the city its unique charm and its romantic atmosphere.

Delicate palazzos have sprung along the Grand Canal since the days of the barbarians, under the powerful reign of the Republic of Venice, which remained strong and independent for nearly a millennium. Throughout those same years, writers, artists, and romantics of every kind came to Venice to be inspired, and have produced a massive body of work singing the praise of the city. But until you come to experience the dream for yourself, walk its narrow cobble stoned streets, along its winding canals, and cross its busy bridges, nothing can prepare you for the wonders of Venice.

HOW TO USE THIS GUIDE

In this pocket guide of Venice, we introduce you to one of the most unique cities in the world. We structure the guide around the city, giving you information on how to get to Venice from abroad, or from other parts of Italy. From there, we introduce all the most important sights and experiences in Venice, some of the best and best-valued restaurants, and the hotels we wholeheartedly recommend. You can plan your entire days with these resources, or follow our signature two-day itinerary, which allows you to hit all the must-see spots, and enjoy the authentic local flavor of Venice.

If you have a few more days, we suggest leaving Venice for the Veneto region, which is full of historically and culturally rich cities, all dating back to the Ancient Roman times. Places like Verona and Padova are great options for a day trip.

Finally, we give you more practical information on Italy, like whether you need a **visa**, the **best time to visit Venice, currency exchanges**, and **culture good-to-knows**. We also include **useful**

Italian phrases at the end of this book. Armed with these, you'll have less to worry about, and more time to enjoy your trip!

Top Experiences in Venice

Venetian Canals

1. Get Lost in Venetian Canals

Canals are the marvels that make Venice what it is – a magical city built on water. Sit by a canal for a meal, or take a boat ride down one of them.

2. Ride in a Gondola, Vaporetto, or Water Taxi Down the Grand Canal

Do this at sunset, and swoon in the romantic atmosphere of the Grand Canal, flanked on both sides by old Venetian buildings, and the sun setting in the distance.

a gondola

3. Visit San Marco Square

Admire the 360 degrees of beauty around you in the most popular piazza in Venice. Both St. Mark's Basilica, a Byzantine treasure, and the famous Doge's Palace, are located in this square.

4. See the Explosion of Color in the Burano Archipelago Near Venice.

Take a day trip to Burano, another island in the lagoon, where rainbow-colored homes fill the island, as if coming out of a child's dream.

5. Watch the Sunset while Sitting on a Bridge

Visit the less touristy districts of Cannaregio or Dorsoduro. Eat an authentic dinner, get a gelato cone after, and watch the sunset over Venice while sitting on one of the ancient bridges in these quarters.

6. See Venice during Carnevale

It may be one of the most crowded and hectic situations you'll ever be in, complete with masses of people donning the colorful Venetian masks, but the experience is also once-in-a-lifetime.

Venetian masks during Carnevale

7. Opera at the Arena in Verona

You can enjoy opera, ballet, and symphonies year-round in Verona, but only in the summer are operas staged in the city's most magnificent venue – the ancient Roman arena.

8. Live la dolce vita !

Il dolce far niente – "the sweetness of doing nothing" is an art form the Italians have long learned to master. So when in Italy, do as the Italians do – celebrate life's pleasures, relax and let the sweetness of life sink in. Eat well, drink well, admire the beauty all around you, and enjoy!

Best of Venice Itinerary

2-Day Itinerary

Day 1

Head to San Marco Square first thing in the morning, as it is the most popular attraction and gets quickly crowded later in the day. Visit the Doge's Palace and St. Mark's Basilica, both located on the square.

From there, head to Rialto Market and the Rialto Bridge. Have lunch nearby while enjoying the beautiful view of the Grand Canal. Try cicchetti – Italian small plates - with a glass of white wine at a cicchetteria.

After lunch, take a gondola or waterbus ride along the Grand Canal. Explore either Dorsoduro or Cannaregio districts. Both of these are less packed with tourists, and equally beautiful with authentic local flavor. Find dinner at a local spot off-the-beaten-path. Prices are sure to be more affordable than near San Marco.

Day 2

Get lost! Literally, wander the streets of Venice and explore different districts from your Day 1 itinerary. Museum fans may want to see the Peggy Guggenheim Museum. La Fenice Opera House is also a worthwhile visit. Use the rest of the day for a day trip to nearby islands of Murano and/or Burano, both offering brightly colored local residences.

3-Day Itinerary

Day 1 and Day 2

Follow itinerary above.

Day 3

You should be able to see most of the top attractions on the Venice Lagoon during the first two days of your visit here. If you have an extra day, we suggest taking a day trip into the rest of the Veneto region, which is fascinating and quite different from Venice and its overdeveloped tourism. Trains run frequently.

Verona, about one and a half hour away by train, and Padova, 30 minutes away, are both good options.

VENICE

There is simply no place like Venice. This sanctuary is an island located on a lagoon is as lovely as it was six hundred years ago despite heavy tourism – 56,000 residents and 20 million tourists per year – and has retained its romantic charm. Once called the Most Serene Republic of Venice, Venice dates back to 827 AD, and has prospered through the century as an Italian city state under the rule of a Roman-style Senate, headed by the Doge.

Venice is divided into districts known as "sestieri". Most of your sightseeing will be in the sestieri of Cannaregio, Castello, Dorsoduro, San Polo, Santa Croce, and San Marco, which together make up the old city center. There are no cars here, as the city is easily walkable. Strolling, you can get from one side of Venice to the other in a matter of hours. And of course, within the main tourist districts, you'll have the opportunity to take a gondola ride, quite romantic, even if it does not get you to your destination in a hurry.

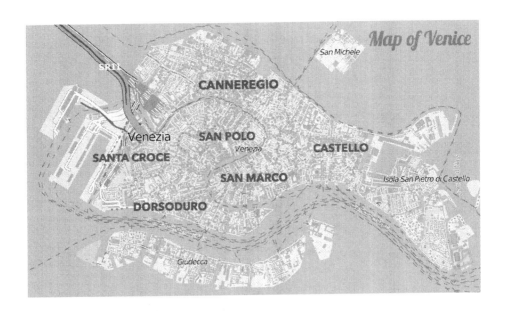

San Marco
San Marco is the center of the Venetian old town, and where most attractions are located. You can find the famous St. Mark's Square here, which is lined with elegant historic buildings like St. Mark's Basilica and the Doge's Palace, and expensive cafes, where you can sit, people watch, and enjoy live music in the evening.

San Polo
Connected to San Marco by the Rialto Bridge, San Polo is one of the oldest parts of Venice. At the food of the bridge on the San Polo side, you can find the massive Venice Fish Market, and an

open-air vegetable market that you might consider visiting. The city's medieval roots are still very much visible in this small but pretty district.

Santa Croce

Santa Croce is just next to San Polo along the Grand Canal. It is one of the oldest parts of the city as well, and less touristy.

Cannaregio

Across from the Grand Canal from Santa Croce is Cannaregio, a large district that starts with Santa Lucia train station and ends with the Rialto Bridge. You'll find many canals in Cannaregio, including the second largest in Venice, the Cannaregio Canal, along with beautiful squares and plenty of local residents. This is a good district to visit for some off-the-beaten-path, authentic, local cuisine without the tourist premium.

Dorsoduro

Located across the Accademia Bridge from San Marco, and home to the Accademia Museum and Guggenheim Art Collection, Dorsoduro is another good off-the-beaten-path district. The walkway along the Guidecca Canal is very tranquil.

Castello

Castello is home to the Arsenale, the old shipyard of Venice and today an interesting museum. You can walk around, away from the tourist bustle of San Marco, and catch the boats for the Murano and Burano Islands here.

Sights

Saint Mark's Basilica (Basilica di San Marco)

Located on the Piazza San Marco, Saint Mark's Basilica is one of Venice's top attractions. This impressively stunning building is renowned worldwide for its large collection of priceless artifacts, and a seemingly endless supply of secret places with a storied past. Do not miss the symbol of the basilica – the Greek Hellenistic sculpture, the gilded bronze horses.

As with most churches in Italy, you should dress appropriately to gain entrance. No short skirts or bare shoulders allowed, and the same applies to large backs or rucksacks (you'll have to deposit them around the corner from the main entrance.

St. Mark's Basilica

Doge's Palace (Palazzo Ducale)
This beautiful palace once served as the residence for Venice's doges, who were the supreme authority of the former Republic. It

is adorned by art throughout, designed to display the wealth and power of the rulers of Venice.

You can get regular tickets either at the Palace, or across the square at the Museo Correr. But consider joining the Secret Itinerary guided tour for €20, which lets you discover secret parts of the palace where the city's administration held office, as well as Casanova's jail and the five hundred year old roof structure.

Doge's Palace

Correr Museum

Included in the €16 ticket to the Doge's Palace, the Correr Museum has a vast and interesting collection of globes, the oldest from the 16th century. Also of interest are a library hall, an archeological museum of Roman antiques, and an important picture gallery. After you finish touring the building, visit the art café that is part of the museum, and enjoy an espresso at one of their tables on San Marco Square.

Bell Tower of St. Mark (Campanile di San Marco)

Climb to the top of the tower for great views of Venice and the lagoon. The current tower is a replica of a much older structure, which collapsed in 1902.

Bell Tower of St. Mark

Rialto Bridge (Ponte di Rialto)

This widely recognized bridge is one of the city's major icons, and dates back 800 years. The first bridge at the site was a wooden structure that collapsed in 1524, while the current bridge was completed in 1591.

Rialto Bridge

La Fenice Theater (Teatro La Fenice)

Although this theater is a 2003 reconstruction, its opulent golden decorations will still impress. Take a walk inside with an audio guide, and learn about the historical structure that burned down in 1996.

Scuola Grande di San Rocco

This old guild house is an exquisite example of Manierist art at its best, and a masterpiece of Tintoretto. Look up to admire the highlight of the building – the ornate ceiling mirrors that are art pieces in their own right.

St. Mary of the Friars Church (Basilica di Santa Maria Gloriosa dei Frari)

Standing on the Campo dei Frari at the heart of the San Polo district, St. Mary of the Friars is one of the greatest churches in the entire city, and a foremost example of the Italian Gothic style. The imposing brick edifice boasts of the second tallest campanile (bell tower) in the city, just after the one in San Marco Square, and it is host to many fine monuments and paintings. You'll want to find the "Assunta" by Titian, the most prominent painter of the 16th Century Venetian school.

San Giacomo di Rialto

This church dates to around 421, and is possibly the oldest surviving church in Venice today. You can recognize it by the 15th century clock just above the entrance, red pillars, and beautiful gold accents around the church's exterior.

Peggy Guggenheim Museum

Spawning from a personal collection of modern art of the American heiress Peggy Guggenheim, who came from the Guggenheim family, married modern artist Max Ernst, and funded a number of her husband's contemporaries, this museum is home to works by important modernist artists like Picasso, Kandinsky, Tanguy, Duchamp, Ollock, Dali, and Mondrian. There is also a pretty sculpture garden. Ticket is €12, €10 for seniors, and €7 for students.

Ca' Rezzonico

This museum attempts to recreate the domestic atmosphere of Venetian nobility in the 18th century with room after room of the opulence typical to the wealthy of those days. The effect is interesting, but similar to the displays at the 18th century Venetian palazzos on the Canal Grande.

Jewish Ghetto

Venice's ghetto was the first of that name – the word came from a Venetian word for the Iron Foundry that was on the same site of the Venetian ghetto previously. Eventually, the name came to mean any neighborhood that is made up of a single ethnic or racial group. Today, the Jewish community in the area is thriving, with five synagogues and a variety of shops, restaurants, and other Jewish establishments. Visiting the area on Saturdays or late Fridays, the Jewish Sabbath, and you'll be greeted by ghostly streets void of locals.

Experience

Take a Water Bus, Water Taxi or Gondola

Each of these water transportations down the Grand Canal offers a side of Venice that is not visible from the streets – amazing architecture flank the water, basking in soft seaside sunlight, while a fascinating parage of Venetian watercraft pass you by.

The Vaporetto water buses cost €7, which is not cheap but still more affordable than gondola rides, which will cost about €80 after some haggling with your gondolieres. You might be able to drive the price down more if several of them are chasing after you.

Explore the Maze That Is Venice and Get Lost
Head to the quieter, less touristy Cannaregio or Dorsoduro sestiere, and meander along their winding cobble stone streets, to get to know the authentic Venice. Allow yourself to get lost, and

you may just spot a lovely view, framed by the colorful facades of old Venetian buildings, that no guidebook can tell you about. Best of all, you will be able to enjoy it without having to jostle with the crowd.

Regata 'Storica

If you are lucky enough to be in town on the first Sunday of every September, you will be treated to the historic fleet event that displays nearly 100 varieties of Venetian boats from the city's storied past, including large oarships from the Roman Empire and Medieval times, rowing down the Grand Canal. There are several races during the day as well, featuring brightly painted gondolini, which make excellent photo opportunities and even better memories.

Carnival of Venice

One of the most popular carnivals in the world, Venice's annual carnival is especially appreciated for the unusual and elaborate masks worn by its participants.

Island Hopping around Venice

Boat services take you to the islands around Venice.

Shopping

Being a major tourist destination, Venice has a flourishing souvenir shopping scene. You can find little stores everywhere, stocked with local specialties like Carnival masks, and marbled paper. Prices vary wildly, so be sure to compare before buying, and try to stay away from places like St. Mark's Basilica.

Eat and Drink

Tourism has driven up food prices in Venice, along with lodging and everything else. Steer away from San Marco and other crowded streets. Instead, head to Dorsoduro area on the south side of the city, where locals and students go to eat for cheap. Of course, you may still wish to participate in the quintessential Venetian experience, and dine beside the canal, but be prepared to splurge for it.

As with many Italians, Venetians meet before dinner for happy hour, which is called "bacari" here. Head to an osteria, and sample typical aperitifs like "spritz", which is a cocktail made of Prosecco wine and Aperol or Campari, while munching on small plates of "cicchetti" – Venetian tapas. These might include small triangular sandwiches, bite-sized rolls with cold cuts, fried balls of minced fish or meat, or meat cooked on a spit.

Bellini is a delicious mixture of white peach juice and Prosecco, that ubiquitous Venetian Champagne-like sparkling wine. It was invented right here in Venice, at a place called Harry's Bar.

Dal Moro's Fresh Pasta-To Go
$
Italian
Just off of St. Mark's Square, this convenient take-out pasta restaurant is perfect for a quick and affordable bite between sightseeing in the center of Venice. But don't let the low prices fool you – the food is nothing but fresh and delicious. There is a small bar inside the restaurant too, where you can stand and eat.
Address: Calle de la Casseleria, 5324 | Castello, 30122 Venice

Bacareto Da Lele
$
Italian
Bacareto is a little hole in the wall sandwich restaurant that also has great wine. You'll notice locals and tourists going in and out all day. The sandwiches are cheap and tasty, made with fresh bread pressed to perfection. Try the mortadella pannini.
Address: Campo dei Tolentini 183 - Santa Croce, Venice, Italy

Antico Forno
$

Italian

Located on the way to and from Rialto Bridge, this small place offers quick service, good prices, and outstanding pizza. You can take your pick of thick or thin crust. There are only 2 or 3 seats, so most customers will get their food to go. Capricciosa, prosciutto, and funghi are all great choices.
Address: Ruga Vecchia San Giovanni (Ruga Rialto), 30125 Venice

Cocaeta
$

Crepes

If you want a break from pasta and pizza, try Cocaeta, which serves authentic and delicious crepes, both savory and sweet. The menus are available in English. You can choose from a variety of ingredients, or combine a few for your own concoction.
Address: Cannaregio 548 B, 30121 Venice

Hostaria Vecio Biavarol
$$

Cichetteria

In a city filled with tourist traps, Hostaria Vecio Biavarol is a breath of fresh air. Rather than a restaurant, this is a place to try some great wine and cocktails, with a few delicious small plates. The cheese and meat plate is especially good.
Address: Fondamenta Dei Tolentini, 225 | Sestiere Santa Croce, 30135 Venice

Osteria Alla Ciurma
$$

Italian

A great place to sample Italian wine in Venice, Osteria Alla Ciurma is a cozy place that serves affordable and delicious food as well. The restaurant is small and located on an inconspicuous side street, so you may have slight difficulty finding it, but the

work will be well worth it. Each small plate is only one to three euros, and they are actually very sizeable for small plates!
Address: Calle Galeazza 406 | Sestiere San Polo 406, 30125, Venice

El Refolo
$$
Italian

Many locals favor this bar and restaurant for great and reasonably priced drinks – sparkling rose and birra piccolo are both good – and delicious snacks. Try the plate of pork, cooked to perfection.
Address: Via Garibaldi - Castello 1580, 30122 Venice

Osteria Enoteca Ai Artisti
$$$
Italian

Roughly translated to "Artists' Restaurants", Osteria Enoteca Ai Artisti composes their plates with the same care and dedication artists compose their canvases. The menu changes here everyday, depending on what fresh ingredients can be found that day, all paired with great local wine. Fish pasta of any kind will be great here.
Address: Fondamenta della Toletta Dorsoduro, 1169/A, 30123, Venice

Impronta Cafe
$$$
Italian

You'll be taken care of at this beautiful restaurant if you want to splurge on dinner while in Venice. Food is delicious and artfully arranged. You'll love the starter, which is actually composed of seven small portions of different kinds of fish and seafood. For the main course, try duck leg, or bacon-wrapped steak. There is also a cheaper lunch menu if you'd rather drop by midday.
Address: Dorsoduro 3815/3817, 30123 Venice

Ristorante Alla Corone

$$$$
Italian
Make a reservation ahead of time at Ristorante Alla Corone. You won't regret it! The food is some of the best to be had in Venice – fresh, hot, and very creative.
Address: Campo della Fava 5527 | Castello, 30122 Venice

Stay

Hotel Moresco
Address: Sestiere Dorsoduro 3499, 30123 Venice, Italy

The Gritti Palace
Address: Campo Santa Maria del Giglio 2467, 30124 Venice, Italy

Al Ponte Antico Hotel
Address: Calle dell'Aseo | Cannaregio 5768, 30131 Venice, Italy

Ca'Maria Adele
Address: Dorsoduro 111 | Rio Terra dei Catecumeni, 30123 Venice, Italy

Corte Di Gabriela
Address: Calle Avvocati 3836 S. Marco, 30124 Venice, Italy

Hotel Ai Cavalieri di Venezia
Address: Calle Borgolocco 6108, Castello, 30122 Venice, Italy

Hotel Canal Grande
Address: Campo San Simeone Grande, 30135 Venice, Italy

Hotel Antiche Figure
Address: Santa Croce, 687 | Fondamenta S. Simeon Piccolo, 30135 Venice, Italy

Hotel Al Ponte Mocenigo
Address: S. Croce 2063, 30135 Venice, Italy

Charming House DD724
Dorsoduro 724, 30123 Venice, Italy

Getting in

By Air
You can fly directly into Marco Polo Airport, which is located on the mainland near Mestre – technically part of the city of Venice, but not what everyone considers Venice which is in the lagoon.

Once you land, you can take either an "Alilaguna" waterbus directly from the airport (€15 for a 75 minute boat trip), to get to the island of Venice. There are three routes taking you different parts of Venice. Alternatively, you can take a bus from the airport to Piazzale Roma, the main bus station on Venice Lagoon.

If cost is not a concern, you can hire a speedy water taxi, which gets you to Venice in 30 minutes for about €110.

By Train

If you are visiting other parts of Italy like Rome or Florence, it is much easier to take the train to Venice, since the train station, Venezia Santa Lucia, is directly located at the lagoon.

Getting Around

By Foot

Venice is a very walkable city, since cars are entirely absent. The districts you'll want to visit are all close to each other – you can walk from one end to the other in about an hour., don't rush yourself, since a major part of Italian life is to relax and not rush. Allow yourself the leisure to meander and get lost. It's an experience in itself!

Water Bus and Water Taxies

If you don't feel like walking much, or want to get around more quickly, you can take the waterbuses. Strangely, the service routes change frequently, so it is advisable to get an updated map from your hotel. One waterbus ride is €7 – quite pricy – so it may be more economical to purchase a travel pass. Your options are 12 hours for €18; 24 hours for €20; and 36 hours for €25.

Water taxies are also available for hire. As taxies on land, these can add up pretty quickly.

Gondolas

A visit to Venice is not complete without a gondola ride along the canals at sunset. Think of these as sightseeing rides complete with talent shows from your entertaining driver instead of a practical option to get you somewhere.

Venice Card Saving Pass

This saving pass is only a good idea if you are in Venice for more than a few days. When you purchase, you can choose from various options that gives you combined and discounted access to public transportation, cultural attractions, public bathrooms, and the waterbuses, etc. However, most of the top attractions are not included in the Venice Card, so you should not purchase it unless you have around a week, and want to explore the island at a leisurely pace. You'll discover some hidden gems this way.

OTHER ISLANDS

The Venetian Lagoon is an enclosed bay of the Adriatic Sea. Aside from Venice, the lagoon is also home to the city of Chioggia at the southern inlet, Lido di Venezia and Pellestrina, which are considered parts of Venice, and a number of other inhabited and uninhabited islands.

The most famous of which is Murano, which is known for colorful glass, and Burano, famous for lace, as well as its picturesque streets and houses, each painted a different shade of pastel.

To commute between the islands, you can take the vaporetti (water buses) and water taxis. Both can get you from one part of the lagoon to another.

Murano

Referring to a series of islands linked by bridges in the Venetian Lagoon, the town of Murano is most famous for its long tradition of artisan glass production. The Grand Canal splits the small island into two parts, which all together are only about one mile across. So take a day trip from Venice by waterbus, and explore on foot – you'll discover beautiful colors, little shops where you can purchase delicate souvenirs, and many restaurants.

From Venice, Murano is just 10 to 25 minutes by waterbus, depending on which stop you want to get off.

Murano Glass

Sights

Church of Santa Maria e San Donato (Chiesa dei Santi Maria e Donato)

This church is famous for its 12th century Byzantine mosaic pavement, which is similar to the floor of the Basilica di San Marco in Venice. There is also the mosaic dome in the apse of the Virgin Mary, which is home to the legendary bones of the dragon slain by Saint Donatus, who lent the church his name. Like most churches, there is a bell tower separate from the main building in this church.

Church of St. Peter the Martyr (Chiesa di San Pietro Martire)

Edificated in 1348, the Church of St. Peter the Martyr was originally dedicated to St. John the Baptist. The building was burnt to the ground in the 1400s, and rebuilt to its current appearance in 1511. It houses artworks including a Baptism of Christ attributed to Tintoretto, Assumption with Saints and Barbarigo Altarpiece, both of which were done by Giovanni Bellini.

Glass Museum

Housed in the large Palazzo Giustinian near island center, the Museo Vetrario pays homage to the island's long history of glassmaking production with a century-by-century tour of Venetian glassmaking.

Glass Factories

Known as "fornaci" in Italian, some of these glassworks date back to the medieval time. Most are open to the public, and give tours and demonstrations that showcase the unique artistry of the Murano glassmakers.

Burano

About 40 minutes away from Venice by waterbus is the island of Burano. It is known for its small, brightly painted houses, very popular with artists who take up residence here and work on their art. These houses are highly valued by the government, and anyone who wishes to paint their home must first apply for permission – only certain colors are allowed for each lot to preserve the overall aesthetic of the island.

Burano is also known for its long history of lacemaking. Be sure to check out the shops for small locally woven lace souvenirs.

Lido

The island of Lido, just 10 minutes by waterbus from Venice, is actually a long sandbar in the Venetian lagoon. If you wish to have a more authentic and less touristy experience in the lagoon, visit this underrated gem in lieu of the more popular Burano and Murano islands. It is trendier than Venice, not to mention more residential, and may feel familiar to a place like Palm Beach in Florida with its many upscale homes and historic architecture.

Experiences

Enjoy the Beach
Lido has the nicest beaches and seascape in the entire lagoon, hands down, which is why the rich and famous have their upscale houses on this island. Most of the beachfront is owned by the

various hotels, but if your hotel does not offer beach access, you may still use the public beach at the end of the Gran Viale, which can get a bit crowded.

Sporting Activities
One of the best ways to explore the island is to rent a bike from one of the many shops at the Gran Viale. You can also golf and play tennis on Lido, which has that relaxed and leisurely island feel. If you don't feel like sweating, stroll along the quiet streets and window shop.

Voga Longa
This annual rowing regatta takes place on Lido in late May each year. It is essentially a marathon on water – serious competitors row 32 kilometers under 3.5 hours in order to receive a certificate of attendance. However, anyone with a human-powered water vessel is welcome to participate, and some foreign teams take up 10 hours to complete the whole race, just for the fun of it.

The original purpose of the race, established in 1974, was to protest the increasing use of powerboats in Venice. But it has since grown into a veritable festival, attracting over 1,500 vessels with up to 5,500 racers each year. It is a nice way to see the lagoon as well, since the racetrack visits different parts of Venice and various nearby islands. Locals and visitors alike line up alongside the canals to cheer for the racers.

Note that the race, no matter how long it takes you to compete, is still physically demanding. Visitors wishing to participate should be very experienced in rowing or sculling, and practice ahead of time. It is a marathon!

Venice International Film Festival
Part of the Venice Biennale, the famous film festival takes place in late August or early September on the island of Lido every year. Screenings are held in the historic Palazzo del Cinema, and

other beautiful venues nearby. It is the most prestigious international film festival in the world.

VERONA

Situated an hour away from Venice in Italy's Veneto region, Verona earned its fame as the setting of Shakespeare's most famous star-crossed lovers – Romeo and Juliet – met their heart-wrenching end. Less touristy and crowded than Venice, Verona offers a more relaxed atmosphere where you can wander in peace.

The city dates back more than two thousand years. In the first century AD, it came under Roman rule, the evidence of which can still be seen in many ruins, most notably the Arena, which looks like a copy of Rome's Colosseum. There are also evidence of Austrian occupation in the 12th to 14th centuries, when the powerful Scaligery family ruled over Verona, in the city's fortifications and the family emblem, a ladder, on architectures across the city.

Sights

The Arena
This enormous Roman amphitheater is crumbling on the outside, but still retains its elliptical shape erected in the first century AD. It is the world's third-largest amphitheater to survive from antiquity, though much of its outer ring was damaged during an earthquake in 1117. You can still catch an opera performance here today during the summer season.

Piazza Bra
The largest Piazza in Verona, Piazza Bra is filled with cafes and restaurants where you can sit and relax. The Palazzo Barbieri, which is the town hall of Verona, along with several other notable buildings including the Arena, also occupy the parameter.

Piazza delle Erbe
The piazza served as the Roman forum in ancient times, and is still a focal point of the city today. On the square you can find the "Britney Verona" fountain, the 14th century Gardello Tower, and a market that is, admittedly, rather touristy.

Basilica of St. Zeno (Basilica di San Zeno Maggiore)
Located slightly off city center, this basilica is rich in devotional artwork and historical preservation. The church is dedicated to fourth century North African priest Zeno, who was ordained Bishop of the city in 363, and has become the city's patron saint after his death. The body of Zeno lies in the church's undercroft, with a Medieval statue of the saint watching over the grounds in full episcopal robes, dangling a golden fish at the end of a fishing rod, paying homage to his humble start in life.

Juliet's House (Casa di Guilietta)
Here is reputedly where Shakespeare's lovely heroine leaned from the balcony, speaking with her lover below. The house is

especially popular with love-struck teenagers who take photos in a similar position as Romeo and Juliet.

In reality, the house has no connection with the Bard's fictional characters, though it is indeed an old structure. The city added the balcony in 1936, and declared the house Juliet's to attract tourists. More discerning visitors can still enjoy a small collection of Renaissance frescos.

Juliet's Balcony

Castelvecchio
This 14-century castle is currently an art museum that is packed with medieval sculpture and Renaissance paintings. Children enjoy running around castle fortifications and the extensive ramparts, while the parents can look over from the adjoining bridge for some fantastic views of the castle on the river.

Castel Vecchio Bridge
Attached to Castelvecchio, this unusual pedestrian bridge is built with red brick in its upper part – like all landmarks dating from

the Scaliger era – and with white marble on the bottom. It was built in 1354 by the Scalinger ruling family to defend the Veronese, and could be used as an escape route in the event of unrest.

The bridge, along with Ponte Pietra, were completely destroyed by retreating Nazi troops in 1945, but local volunteers rebuilt them brick by brick to their present states.

Ponte Pietra

This arch bridge, built over the Adige on the northeastern part of the old city, dates back to 100 BC to the Roman Republic. Over 2,000 years later, retreating Nazis blew it up. Locals fished the rubble out of the river later, and pieced the bridge back together over 10 years. As such, only the arch closest to the city is an original Roman arch. You can take in a great view of the old theater and the town from the bridge.

Sant'Anastasia

This impressive basilica took over 250 years to construct, and one look at its beautiful façade, you'll understand why. The interior of the church is even more breathtaking – even the floor is beautiful with its intricate patterns in three different types of marble, each with a unique color.

Piazzale Castel San Pietro

Ascend the long flight of stairs, lined by pretty old houses on both sides, and you'll be at the top of Verona – the old town spreads before your eyes in all its splendor. Nowhere in Verona offers the same view of the narrow streets and tall church towers like this piazzale, so the climb is quite worth it!

Experiences

Sweeping Views

The best view of the city can be had from the top of Castel San Pietro, which towers over the rooftops that glimmer under the sun.

Shopping at Verona's Golden Mile
Via Mazzini, between Piazza Bra and Piazza delle Erbe, is known as Verona's Golden Mile, where you can find most of the major Italian labels. If you are not prepared to drop the big bucks, it can still be fun to window shop and people watch.

Eat

Verona boasts of a strange local delicacy – horsemeat. Try Pastissada de caval, an ancient horsemeat stew that is tender and flavorful with a myriad of herbs and vegetable, served with polenta. For those not keen on eating horses, Brasato all'Amarone is a braised beef dish cooked with Amarone wine, also served with polenta.

Veronese "bollito misto" is also very good. This mixed meat dish popular across northern Italy, known as "lesso" here, is topped with a special sauce – made from meat stock, grated stale bread, ox marrow, and abundant black pepper – only found here in the city. It is traditionally served at Christmas time, but now can be found year round.

Zio Lele
$
Pizza
Pizza at Zio Lele is made fresh daily, and served by weight rather than by slice or pie. You'll have your pick of many toppings, but the courgette and brie are both recommended by locals. The proprietor of the place speaks English, and is very friendly.
Address: Via Santa Maria Rocca Maggiore 6a, 37129 Verona, Italy

Osteria Il Ciottolo

$$

Italian

Osteria Il Ciottolo serves traditional Veronese cuisine, with products sourced locally. The serving staff is friendly, so ask for their recommendations. The cuisine of the region is usually hearty and a bit more rustic than in major cities.

Address: Corso Cavour 39 C, 37121 Verona, Italy

Osteria Da Morandin

$$

Italian

Serving authentic local cuisine with interesting ingredients, Osteria Da Morandin is known for its donkey ragu, horsemeat stew, salted fish, and beef carpaccio, among other delicacies. The restaurant is divided into two sections: a bar at the front that serves small plates paired with local wine, while the back is a sit-down restaurant that can seat 20 to 25 people. For dessert, try tiramisu, for which the pastry chef tried 10 different types of mascarpone before settling on the right one. What is more, Osteria Da Morandin is great value for your money. Hearty pasta dishes are around 5 euros, main dishes around 7 to 9 euros, wine is 2.5 euros per glass, 15 per bottle.

Via 20 Settembre, 144, 37129 Verona VR, Italy

Enoteca Segreta

$$$

Italian

Locals love Enoteca Segreta, and you will too. Like the rest of Verona, the restaurant is romantic and quiet, especially if you get a table in the garden. The food is incredibly fresh, and includes a selection of duck and goose "salumi" sausages, served with pear, arugula, and cheeses. You wouldn't believe the flavor explosion!

Address: Vicolo Samaritana, 37100 Verona, Italy

La Griglia

$$$

Italian

Address: Via Leoncino, 29, 37121 Verona, Italy

We went to La Griglia based on TripAdvisor reviews and were not disappointed. When we arrived all the outside tables were occupied but several seemed close to leaving and the Maitre d' told us a couple of minutes, so we waited and sat down shortly afterwards.

The food was excellent; huge, tender, juicy fillet steaks for a very reasonable price. Good advice on local wines; we were recommended a young Valpolicella for 26 Euros which was delightful.

The Maitre d' and our waiter were attentive without being intrusive....oh, and did I mention the huge, tender, juicy fillet steaks!

Getting In

From Venice, the train ride to Verona only takes about one hour. You'll get off at Verona Porta Nuova, the main trains tation in Verona. From there, you can take a walk down a long boulevard to reach town center, where the Arena is located. It takes about 15 minutes, and offers a great first view of the city.

PADOVA (PADUA)

The ancient city of Padova is located in the northern part of Italy. It has been inhabited since Roman times, and became a strategically and culturally important city-state over 500 years ago during the Renaissance. Today, it remains the economic and communications hub of the province of Padova. There is plenty of art and history for those who haven't had enough from Venice, as well as Europe's largest square for those wanting to return to the modern world!

Sights

Scrovegni Chapel (Cappella degli Scrovegni)
Just to the north of city center is Scrovegni Chapel, where Giotto's frescoes cover the walls and ceilings. Aside from being beautiful, these frescoes were technically ahead of their time. First built in 1303 to 1305, the chapel is remarkably well-preserved.

Note that due to the popularity of the sight and the frailty of its art, visitors are required to buy tickets ahead of time – same day tickets are very rarely sold. Entry is tightly monitored, and only 25 people are allowed in at a time in order to preserve the ideal inside temperature to protect the frescoes. You are only allowed inside for 25 minutes, and will not be allowed to photograph.

Basilica del Santo (Basilica di Sant'Antonio)
The most famous site in Padova, St. Anthony's Basilica attracts millions of pilgrims every year. The building dates back to the 1200s, just after Saint Anthony's death, and is home to his tomb and relics from his life. Donatello is credited for the statues and crucifix on the main altar, as well as the statue of the horse.

Prato della Valle
A massive 90,000 square meters, Prato della Valle is the largest square in Europe, and frequently hosts concerts, fairs, and a giant market on Saturdays. The ground was historically a Roman theater, becoming a fairground at a later time, and was converted to its present form in 1775. It is also likely the world's most beautiful such urban square, with a large central grassy area, a statue-lined canal surround the area, and most importantly, an expanse of flagstones separate the modern day hubbub from the peaceful park, for visitors' enjoyment. You'll see many local joggers, bikers, and rollerbladers, while you relax in the evening, after dinner.

Duomo
The Duomo of Padova may be relatively small compared to duomos you see elsewhere in Italy, but its small façade fronts one of the most intricately designed buildings you'll see in the country, designed by none other than Michelangelo himself. Inside, there are modern touches that surprise the visitor amid statues and artworks. '

The baptistery of the Duomo is filled with frescoes in late medieval style, including works of Giusto de Menabuoi, completed between 1375 and 1376.

University of Padova
The University of Padova, built in 1222, is the second oldest university in Italy and among the earliest universities in the world. Galileo gave lectures here – you can still visit the same room. Today, it remains one of the best universities in Italy. You can take a guided tour, and visit the world's olest anatomical theater, and "Aula di Medicina", the original medical lecture hall.

Botanical Garden of Padova
The world's very first botanical garden, the Botanical Garden of Padova has been on the UNESCO World Heritage list since 1997. The small garden is artfully laid out, so that visitors have the impression of peace and solitude, even though the garden is a popular tourist destination. Important exhibits include the carnivorous plants, and the wooded hill at the southeast corner with a double helix pair of paths.

Roman Ruins
Like Verona and Rome, Padova has the ruins of the old Roman city, including an arena. While not as imposing as its counterparts in larger cities, the Padovan ruin is a pleasant park in which you can glimpse a bit of the city's ancient history. About three quarters of the arena walls still remain today, the rest having been removed to make way for the Scrovegni Chapel and Palace. In the summer, the arena becomes an open-air movie theater. The park is

a very apt representation of the city of Padova, where old and new mix together.

Eat and Drink

Like most Italian cities, Padova has a happy hour tradition called spritz or aperitif. Starting between 7 and 8 in the evening, locals and tourists alike begin to gather in one of the central piazzas – Piazzo delle Erbe, Piazza della Frutta, or Piazza dei Signori – and take advantage of the cheaper drinks prices. The city has a lot of college students and young people, so happy hour here is very fun.

Likewise, students contributed to the tradition of having lunch on the Prato della Valle, either on the central grassy area, or leaning against the statues along the waterfront. As lunch hour drifts into the afternoon, you'll find some of them lingering in the same area to write, rest, or people watch. Feel free to join them in their leisure.

Pinsa
$
Pizza
Pinsa serves made to order thin crust pizzas with just the right amount of sauce and toppings made with fresh local ingredients. This is a great lunch spot after a visit to the Scrovegni Chapel and Donatello Gallery just 100 meters away. There is a fine beer to go with your pizza, and good coffee for after your meal. Check and make sure they sliced your pizza if you are taking it to go. They deliver too if you are too tired after a day of sightseeing, too.
Address: Corso Garibaldi 13, 35122 Padua, Italy

Enoteca dei Tadi
$$
Italian

Just five minutes away from the main square, Enoteca dei Tadi is run by a small family, offering a limited but interesting menu. The menu is in Italian, but you won't regret ordering the lasagna con fungi.
Address: Via dei Tadi, 16, Padua, Italy

La Folperia
$$
Italian
La Folperia cannot be missed on a visit to Padova. The restaurant serves simple, fresh, and very tasty seafood with an explosion of flavor. You can either opt for seafood cooked to go in an authentic Italian street food setting, or sit in the adjacent café's outside seating area, as long as you order a drink from them. Octopus and baccala mantecato recipes are amazing here. The octopus is boiled and diced, and dressed in a simple basil-olive oil dressing, served with baguette slices. Note that the restaurant is only open between 4 and 8pm.
Address: Piazza della Frutta 1, Padua, Italy

Vecchio Falconiere
$$$
Italian
This upscale restaurant in Padova serves up a great selection of pastas and good drinks. But meat lovers definitely should not miss it. Try the house special, with three courses: Spanish sausage, risotto in a cheese bowl, and the most amazing steak you'll ever eat.
Address: Via Umberto I, 31/1, 35122 Padua, Italy

La Finestra
$$$$
Italian
The risotto here is simply incredible, all served up in a warm and welcoming atmosphere. You should also try the gnocchi.
Address: Via dei Tadi 15, 35139 Padua, Italy

Getting In

It is easiest to travel to Padova from Venice, just 30 minutes away by train. The main train station is Padova Centrale. Once in Padova, it is best and easiest to get around on foot. The historic center is small and very walkable.

BOLOGNA

Most foreign visitors will be familiar with spaghetti Bolognese. While the dish is named after Bologna, it is a poor imitation of the gastronomical delights the city has to offer. Well-known among Italians for its incredible cuisine – considered the best even in this country of amazing food – the city of Bologna is relatively unknown to foreigners.

Aside from its cuisine, known as la cucina Bolognese, this historical city of 380,000 inhabitants is also beautiful second only to Venice, with one of the largest and best-preserved historic centers in Italy. Architecture in the city is noted for its rich palette of terracotta reds, burnt oranges, and warm yellows, while its miles of attractive covered walkways, known as "porticos", are among the most intact in all of Europe.

Sights

Sanctuary of Santa Maria della Vita
This church is famous for "The Lamentation", a life-size terracotta group sculpture by Renaissance artist Niccolò Dell'Arca.

Towers of the Asinelli and Garisenda (Torri degli Asinelli e Garisenda)
The most recognizable landmarks of the city, these astonishing towers were built in the 12th century. Today, Torre degli Asinelli, 97.20 meters tall with 498 steps and an incline of 1.3 meters, is open to public, while Torre del Garisenda, 47 meters tall with a lean of 3 meters, is closed to public.

Basilica di Santo Stefano

Also known as the Seven Churches, this basilica consists of seven interconnected religious buildings dating back to 430 AD. Legend has it that Bishop Petronio, now the patron saint of the city, decided to erect a single building divided into seven parts, which represents the seven places where the Passion of the Christ took place. From the piazza on which it is located, the facades of three churches – the Church of the Calvary, the Church of Saint Vitale, and the Church of Agricola – are visible.

Piazza Maggiore

A large pedestrian square located in the center of the city's old district, Piazza Maggiore is surrounded by the Basilica of San Petronio, the City Hall, the portico del Banchi, and the Palazzo del Podesta.

Basilica di San Petronio

Many of Bologna's treasures can be found here at the Basilica di San Petronio, such as the sundial by Cassini and Guglielmini, which indicates the exact period of the current year at all times, the "S. Rocco" by Parmigianino, and the glittering Bolognini Chapel. The museum is located through the left nave of the basilica, and holds many attractive bas-reliefs.

Fountain of Neptune(Fontana di Nettuno)

This famous fountain, built in 1563 by Tommaso Laureti of Palermo, was later embellished by Giambologna, and is considered one of Bologna's most important cultural symbols.

Fountain of Neptune

St. Luke's Basilica (Santuario di Madonna di San Luca)
This round basilica, built in mid-18th century, offers one of the best panoramic views of the city. Walk along the 666 arches of its unique portico, before heading inside for the famous icon, the Madonna di San Luca.

Experience

Motor Shows and Car Museums
Right before the winter holidays each year, Bologna hosts the Motor Show. You can also visit Ducati, Ferrari, and Lamborghini Museums, for automobile masterpieces from luxury Italian carmakers.

Buy local food
Before flying out, be sure to pick up packaged local food, such as handmade pastas and gorgeous cheeses, far superior to anything you're likely to find back home. There are hundreds of small vendors all around the city. You can also head to the Quadrilatero, an old Medieval food market, framed by Piazza Maggiore, via Rizzoli, via Castiglione, and via Farini, that has been in existence since Roman times.

Cooking Classes
For a fun and practical experience, take a cooking class from some of the best chefs in Italy while you are in Bologna.

Eat

Eating is what you are chiefly in Bologna to do. Generally considered the culinary capital of Italy with its fabulous local produce cooked ingeniously, Bologna is practically incapable of offering a bad meal.

It goes without saying that you should try fresh pasta in the city where many varieties – tortellini, tagliatelle, and lasagna – originated. Trust us, you have not had pasta as they are meant to be until you've tried them here.

The city is also famous for its cured pork. Mortadella is an enormous Italian sausage made from finely ground pork, at least 15% of which is the delicious hard fat from the neck of the pig. It is flavored with black pepper, myrtle berries, nutmeg, and pistachios.

Culatello, the "king" of Italian cured meat, is made from the prized hind leg of pigs, salted, massaged and carefully cured before air-drying for a minimum of one year. It offers a fine, intense flavor that you cannot miss.

Bologna is located in the Emilia-Romagna region, which as a whole is known for amazing food. You can find many regional specialties, such as Parmigiano Reggiano cheese, balsamic vinegar of Modena, and Parma ham, right here in Bologna as well.

Delicious Tortellini

La Tana dell'Orso
$
Piadina

La Tana is the place to go if you're looking for the best balance between taste and value. This place is known for its piadina, a thin Italian flatbread that is folded and stuffed with fresh ingredients. The piadina is a Romagna region specialty and a must-try cheap eat.
Address: Via Portazza 10/c, Bologna

Pizzartist
$
Pizza

As its telling name, Pizzartist is the place to go if you're looking for delicious pizza that is well-priced. Pizzartist has nearly a dozen different toppings out at any given time. The pizzas are flavorful, fresh, and the crispy, think crust is baked to absolute perfection. Address:
Address: Via Marsala, 35/A, Bologna

Cinque 50
Italian, Pasta
$$

This is a place for the pasta lover. As the Emilia-Romagna is known for its fresh-pasta, Cinque 50 is a must-try. Be prepared to have the best tortellini and lasagna of your life. The bruschetta and caprese salad are also worth a mention.
Address: Via Goito 9/2, Bologna

Antica Trattoria Del Reno
Italian, Fusion
$$$$

A phenomenal gustatory experience for the serious foodie, Antica Trattoria Del Reno has a truly creative menu. The owner and Michelin-trained chef dotes a playful twist on Italian cuisine and has changing menus based on seasonal products. Try this place out when you've eaten as much pasta and lasagna as your palate could handle.

Address: Via Del Traghetto 5/3, Bologna

PLANNING YOUR TRIP

BEST TIME TO VISIT VENICE

Venice is at its best in spring and fall, when temperature is pleasantly cool – expect 5°C to 15°C in March – and its canals and cobble stoned streets are not overrun by tourists. Between November and January, it can be quite cold, windy, and damp. It rarely snows in the city, but from December to March, it can be very rainy, especially in the morning. The city gets dark and stormy. Mosquitoes and flies swarm in the street. During these seasons, be careful especially if you are planning to drive in or out, since it can be hazardously foggy. But to make up for the weather, the city is also at its quietest then, and you may find some interesting and unique experiences, and a different side to Venice that most do not get to see.

The worst time to visit, sadly, would be during the annual Carnival, when the city is practically sinking because of the massive crowds that descend for the world's most famous festival. It is an experience to remember, but be mentally prepared.

In the summer – May through mid-September, expect huge hoards of tourists. The picturesque island may not look as beautiful in pictures when crowds block your shot of St. Mark's Basilica.

EXCHANGE RATES

Unit = Euro (€)

Rates are calculated at the time of this writing. Please check before your departure for the up-to-date exchange rate.

USD: 1 Dollar = 0.9 Euro
Canadian Dollar: 1 Dollar = 9.71 Euro
British Pounds: 1 Pound = 1.39 Euro
Australian Dollar: 1 Dollar = 0.67 Euro

VISA INFORMATION

Italy is a member of the Schengen agreement. There are no border controls between countries that have signed the treaty, so citizens from those countries can freely cross into Italy. Many non-EU countries are visa-exempt. Citizens from those countries will only need to produce a valid passport when entering the country, as the stamp counts as a declaration. For more information, visit the Italian Ministry of Foreign Affairs website: http://www.esteri.it/mae/en/ministero/servizi/stranieri/default.htm l.

US: eligible for visa-free stay, up to 90 days
Canada: eligible for visa-free stay, up to 90 days
Australia: eligible for visa-free stay, up to 90 days

ESSENTIAL ITALIAN CULTURE TO KNOW

Italians are in general very patriotic, though people from different regions are proud of their regional heritage as well. They are also more often than not open and friendly, and enjoy interacting with people of every kind. Paying compliments is generally a good way to make friends. For example, tell someone how beautiful his or her town is will work wonders, especially if you can compare their town favorably to another city.

Don't be shy about asking the locals for restaurant recommendations! Italy is filled with good food, and it would be a crime to eat at tourist traps instead of sampling authentic local cuisine. Very often, the locals can point you to their favorite spots off the beaten path, which will be cheaper and more tasty than what you can find on your own in the touristy areas.

Theft is a common problem, especially in large cities like Naples and Rome. Rome is full of pickpocket, though violent crimes are rare. In public areas, crowded metros and buses, hold onto your handbags and wallets. Men should avoid putting their wallets in their back pockets. You should also watch out for gypsies.

USEFUL ITALIAN TERMS AND PHRASES

In larger cities, you'll likely find someone who speaks English, but in a small town or less touristy areas, it'll be helpful to have some Italian phrases.

Do you speak English: Parla Inglese?

Thank You: Grazie.

You are welcome: Prego.

Please: Per favore; Per Piacere.

Good Morning/Good Afternoon: Buon Giorno.

Good Evening: Buona Sera.

Good Night: Buona note.

How are you (singular): Come sta?

How are you (plural): Come state?

Excuse me: Mi scusi/Scusi.

Hello/Goodbye: Ciao.

How much does it cost: Quanto costa?

Where is ...: Dov'è ....?

Lavatory/Toilet: Gabinetto/Bagno.

To eat: Mangiare

Where is the ... Embassy: Dove si trova... l'ambasciata?

Restaurant: Ristorante.

Stamp: Francobollo.

Postcard: Cartolina.

May I take photos: Posso fare fotografie?

Where can I find a...: Dove posso trovare un.../

I have a booking/we have a booking: Ho una prenotazione/Abbiamo una prenotazione.

Would like something to eat: Vorrei qualcosa da mangiare.

I would like something to drink: Vorrei qualcosa da bere.

How can I go to...: Come posso andare a...

I am allergic to...: Sono allergico a...

Do you accept credit cards: Accettate carte di credito?

Prescription: Prescrizione/Ricetta.

May I pay at check-out: Posso pagare al check-out?

Check please: Il conto, per favore.

Is there internet connection: C'è la connessione ad internet.

How much does it cost? / How much does this cost: Quanto costa? / Quanto costa questo?

Police: Polizia/Carabinieri.

Taxi: Taxi.

Bus stop: Fermata dell'autobus.

Airport: Aeroporto.

Train station: Stazione.

Pharmacy: Farmacia.

Doctor: Medico.

Hotel: Albergo/Hotel.

Pain: Dolore.

Blisters: Vesciche.

Food store: Supermercato.

Shop: Negozio.

Hospital: Ospedale.

Emergency room: Pronto soccorso.

Museum: Museo.

Ticket desk: Biglietteria.

Guidebook: Guida turistica.

Guided tour: Visita guidata.

Opening time: Orario di aperture.

Go away: Vai via!

Check out our other Wanderlust Pocket Travel Guides on Italy:

BEST OF ITALY: YOUR #1 ITINERARY PLANNER FOR WHAT TO SEE, DO, AND EAT

BEST OF ROME: YOUR #1 ITINERARY PLANNER FOR WHAT TO SEE, DO, AND EAT

BEST OF FLORENCE AND TUSCANY: YOUR #1 ITINERARY PLANNER FOR WHAT TO SEE, DO, AND EAT

Also available:

BEST OF JAPAN: YOUR #1 ITINERARY PLANNER FOR WHAT TO SEE, DO, AND EAT

BEST OF TOKYO: YOUR #1 ITINERARY PLANNER FOR WHAT TO SEE, DO, AND EAT

BEST OF KYOTO: YOUR #1 ITINERARY PLANNER FOR WHAT TO SEE, DO, AND EAT

CONCLUSION

We hope this pocket guide helps you navigate Venice and find the most memorable and authentic things to do, see, and eat.

Thank you for purchasing our pocket guide. After you've read this guide, we'd really appreciate your honest book review!

Sincerely,
The Wanderlust Pocket Guides Team

CREDITS

Cover design by Wanderlust Pocket Guide Design Team
Map of Venice original source: OpenStreetMap

COPYRIGHT AND DISCLAIMER

Made in the USA
Lexington, KY
03 January 2016

algorithms

Anthony Ralston & Hugh Neill

TEACH YOURSELF BOOKS

For UK orders: please contact Bookpoint Ltd, 78 Milton Park, Abingdon, Oxon OX14 4TD. Telephone: (44) 01235 400414, Fax: (44) 01235 400454. Lines are open from 9.00–6.00, Monday to Saturday, with a 24 hour message answering service. Email address: orders@bookpoint.co.uk

For U.S.A. & Canada orders: please contact NTC/Contemporary Publishing, 4255 West Touhy Avenue, Lincolnwood, Illinois 60646 – 1975, U.S.A. Telephone: (847) 679 5500, Fax: (847) 679 2494.

Long renowned as the authoritative source for self-guided learning – with more than 30 million copies sold worldwide – the *Teach Yourself* series includes over 200 titles in the fields of languages, craft, hobbies, business and education.

British Library Cataloguing in Publication Data
A catalogue record for this title is available from The British Library

Library of Congress Catalog Card Number: 96-071076

First published in UK 1997 by Hodder Headline Plc, 338 Euston Road, London NW1 3BH.

First published in US 1997 by NTC/Contemporary Publishing, 4255 West Touhy Avenue, Lincolnwood (Chicago), Illinois 60646 – 1975 U.S.A.

The 'Teach Yourself' name and logo are registered trade marks of Hodder & Stoughton Ltd.

Typeset by Alden, Oxford, Didcot and Northampton.
Printed in Great Britain for Hodder & Stoughton Educational, a division of Hodder Headline Plc, 338 Euston Road, London NW1 3BH by Cox & Wyman Ltd, Reading, Berkshire.

Impression number   11   10   9   8   7   6   5   4   3

Year   2005   2004   2003   2002   2001   2000

Contents

Preface

Computer science is sometimes defined as 'the study of algorithms'. Thus, knowing something about algorithms is crucial for anyone who wants to learn about computer science. In particular, anyone who wants to write non-trivial programs for a computer must be knowledgeable about algorithms. This book provides an introduction to the study of algorithms which requires no prior knowledge of this subject. It does require some mathematical knowledge but, except in a couple of places, only standard secondary school mathematics.

Although an introduction to the study of algorithms could be presented as a formal academic subject, it seemed to us that, for a book in the *Teach Yourself* series, this subject is best approached informally. We have, therefore, presented the subject of algorithms through a series of examples (in Chapters 3 through 11), each of which concerns an aspect of mathematics or computer science but which is intended specifically to elucidate a particular aspect of the design or analysis of algorithms. These nine chapters are preceded by two introductory chapters which, among other things, present the basic components of the programming-like language we shall use to present all the algorithms in this book. In the last two chapters we discuss, first, the verification of algorithms and then, in the final chapter, consider directly the relationship of algorithms to computer programs.

We would like especially to thank Philip Livermore who made valuable comments on and corrected many errors in an early version of the manuscript. Of course, any errors that remain are our responsibility alone. Please tell us about any you find by sending email to ar9@doc.ic.ac.uk.

Note: Except for three of the figures, this book was prepared entirely using the LaTeX document preparation system and printed from a floppy disk provided by the authors to the publisher. We would like to thank Harris Kwong for his copious advice about LaTeX.

1
Definitions and examples

'Algorithm' is just a fancy word for 'recipe' or 'rule of procedure'. It is derived from the name of a ninth-century Arabic textbook author, Musa al-Khowarizimi (son of Moses, native of Khowarizm). It is a word familiar to – although perhaps quickly forgotten by – generations of secondary school students many of whom have learned the *Euclidean algorithm*, a rule for computing the greatest common divisor of two integers which we shall describe in Chapter 3.

Indeed, algorithms are something most people use every day even when they have never heard of the word. When using a recipe in a cookbook, the algorithm is the specific sequence of instructions (such as 'Add 1 cup of this; add a tablespoon of that; mix and simmer for 10 minutes etc.') which the cook – or chef – follows. Often we use algorithms implicitly, that is, without explicit thought about a sequence of instructions, as in the following example.

■ Example 1.1: The London Underground algorithm

Suppose you wish to travel from station A to station B on the London Underground. (In Fig. 1.1 we have reproduced a portion of the famous map of the Underground.)

Algorithm 1.1 (on page 3) embodies the thought process you might apply in deciding how to make your trip. This algorithm should be understandable even if you have never seen an algorithm before. (By the way, it is only fair that we note that TUBE is not quite correct since there are instances in which it takes more than one change to get from one station to another.)

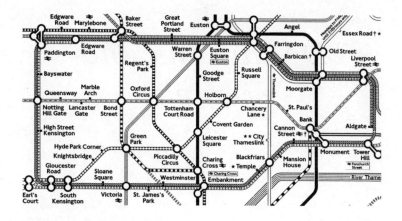

Figure 1.1: A map of the central London portion of the London Underground. Different lines are indicated by different shadings.

In this chapter and the next one, we shall generally rely on your intuitive ability to read algorithms like Algorithm 1.1. However, starting in Chapter 2 and always thereafter, we shall explain precisely the meaning of the constructs in our **algorithmic language** (AL) as we introduce them. Actually, as in TUBE, all algorithms in this book will use a combination of AL (such as **if ... then** in Algorithm 1.1); mathematical notation, which will be explained when it may not be familiar; and ordinary English where this enhances readability. (Appendix 1 summarizes our AL and Appendix 2 summarizes the mathematical notation used in this book.) We shall, as here, uniformly refer to algorithms in the text by their names in small upper-case letters.

You may have noted ambiguities in TUBE (what do you do if two pairs of lines require the same numbers of stops? how about the case where two lines have more than one station in common?). These are not a serious problem with TUBE because it is an algorithm intended for humans who are usually pretty good at resolving ambiguities. We shall, however, strive mightily to avoid any imprecision in all our subsequent algorithms because they are intended to be *executed* (i.e. run or performed) on a computer and computers are notoriously poor at resolving ambiguities.

Input A, B [The two stations]

Algorithm TUBE

> **if** A and B are on the same tube line L
> > **then**
> > travel on line L from A to B
> > > **else** [A and B are on different lines]
> > find all pairs of lines (L_i, L_j) such that
> > A is a station on L_i and B is a
> > station on L_j and the two lines
> > have a station in common.
> > **if** there is only one such pair
> > > **then**
> > > take L_i to a station also on L_j and
> > > then take L_j to station B
> > > > **else** [More than one possible pair]
> > > use pair (L_i, L_j) which requires the fewest stops.
> > **endif**
> **endif**

Output You at station B!

Algorithm 1.1: London Underground

You may have also noticed other ways that TUBE might be improved. (For example, suppose you know a long walk is required to change from one line to another at station C. How might that fact be built into the algorithm?). You should always be on the lookout for ways in which an individual algorithm may be improved. We shall come back to this point from time to time.

Finally, a word about why the subject of Algorithms is important and useful. One specific reason is that algorithms are the basis of all significant computer programs and thus this subject underlies the entire subject of computing and computer science. A more general reason is that the discipline of algorithmic thinking is valuable in carrying out any large enterprise or project because it aids in the planning of such tasks and, in particular, helps avoidance of errors by forcing a consideration of all possibilities. This latter point is crucial when designing a large system (such as a space station), where forgetting even the smallest detail may have life-threatening results.

1 Algorithms in mathematics and computer science

These will be our focus in this book. Indeed, you may have heard the word algorithm used in the context of the 'algorithms of arithmetic' where it refers to those procedures by which uncounted numbers of primary school students have learned to add, subtract, multiply and divide. This use of the word algorithm is emphatically not the one we shall stress in this book because it associates an algorithm with the rote learning of a procedure which is then applied independent of whether the user understands why it works. Our use of the word algorithm in this book will emphasize the design of processes for performing a variety of mathematical and computing tasks, some numeric, some nonnumeric. We shall be particularly interested in processes which can be – and which people want to be – programmed for computers. True, once an algorithm has been well-designed it can be used in rote fashion, but to be used well, an algorithm should always be understood. (If not, it may well be used for something for which it was not designed and for which it gives spurious results.)

Designing an algorithm is not quite enough. You also want to know, assuming it works, how well it works. That is, you want to answer questions such as: How long will it take to do the computation for which it was designed? Can it be modified to be more efficient? Is there perhaps another algorithm which will do the same computation more efficiently? [Note the use of 'computation' here. We use it not just to imply numeric computation but rather any *symbol manipulation* where the symbols could be numbers but could also be letters or, indeed, any other symbols you wish (e.g. pieces on a chessboard).] Answering questions like these is the province of a branch of the study of algorithms called the *analysis of algorithms*. We shall discuss this subject in many places, starting in Chapter 4.

'Assuming it works', we said above. But how do you know if a rule used for anything does what it is supposed to do? Ay, there's the rub! In mathematics and computer science, a *proof* is the only way to assure that something works correctly. With algorithms we speak of their *verification*, a topic we shall introduce briefly in Chapter 12.

A word related to algorithm of which you should be aware is *algorithmics* which refers collectively to the design, analysis and verification of algorithms.

■ Example 1.2: Counting

Our second example is one so simple that it will be very familiar to you: How do you count? That is, given a non-negative integer, what is the next integer in sequence? Now this is so simple, so familiar that your first reaction may be: Why do we need a rule (i.e. an algorithm) at all for such a trivial process? Our answer is that the problem here is not how to count – of course, you know how to do that – but rather whether you can explain how to count to someone (or some*thing* like a computer) who (or which) does not know. That's not quite so easy. Whether or not you can do this is a test of whether you really understand counting. It is a mathematical truism that, if you can explain a piece of mathematics to someone else, than you must understand it yourself. In a computer context, an equivalent statement is that the test of whether you understand a piece of mathematics or computing is whether you can write an algorithm (or program a computer) to perform the task. (In Chapter 13 we shall have more to say about the connection between algorithms and computer programs.) So, before reading any further, think about how you would explain counting to a 'computer' which is so rudimentary that its only arithmetic capability is to be able to add 1 to the digits 0, 1, ..., 8 (but not 9 since adding 1 to 9 involves a carry into the tens place). Figure 1.2 and Algorithm 1.2 are two attempts to explain the idea of counting using this computer. Note first that we represent an integer as an array of digits $D_n D_{n-1} D_{n-2} \ldots D_1 D_0$, so that, for example, 2409 is represented by $D_3 = 2, D_2 = 4, D_1 = 0, D_0 = 9$.

Before reading further, try to decide which figure you prefer. We'll tell you our preference shortly. But first let's analyse these two presentations.

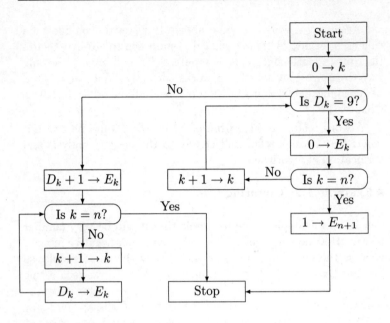

Figure 1.2: Flowchart for adding 1 repeatedly to an integer $I = D_n D_{n-1} D_{n-2} \ldots D_1 D_0$.

1 Both figures implement the idea that, starting from the least significant digit of the non-negative integer I (i.e. the right-hand end), we work left, replacing 9s by 0s until the first digit not equal to 9 appears; this digit is then increased by 1 and all other digits are left unchanged. In the special case in which all the digits of I are 9, they are all changed to zero and a 1 is inserted at the left-hand end. Of course, this special case must be handled if our solution is to be complete. This emphasizes a necessary part of all algorithmic thinking: *All possibilities must be considered.*

2 We think the notation and terminology in both figures will be clear even if you haven't seen things like them before. But, specifically, in Fig. 1.2 notation of the form $a \to b$ means that the value of expression a *replaces* the value of variable b. In Algorithm 1.2 notation of the form $b \gets a$ means precisely the

Input n [Integer greater than 0]

    $D_i, i = 0, 1, \ldots, n$ [Digits of $I = D_n D_{n-1} \cdots D_1 D_0$]

Algorithm COUNTING

    $k \leftarrow 0$ [Initialise digit pointer to 0]

    repeat until $k > n$ **or** $D_k < 9$ [Find first digit not 9]

        $E_k \leftarrow 0$ [Change 9's to 0's]

        $k \leftarrow k + 1$

    endrepeat

    if $k > n$ **then** $E_{n+1} \leftarrow 1$ [I all 9's]

          else $E_k \leftarrow D_k + 1$ [Increase first non-9 digit by 1]

             repeat until $k = n$ [Copy rest of digits]

                $k \leftarrow k + 1$

                $E_k \leftarrow D_k$

             endrepeat

    endif

Output $E_i, I = 0, 1, \ldots, m$ [$I + 1$; $m = n$ or $n + 1$]

Algorithm 1.2: Counting

---

same thing. [A *variable* is a name given to some quantity in a computation. It may consist of any combination of letters and digits and should generally be chosen for a mnemonic reason. An *expression* is any combination of variables, constants, operators (such as $+$, $-$ etc.) and mathematical functions (e.g. $\sin$, $\cos$ etc.) which conforms to the usual mathematical rules for combining such quantities. Computer programming languages usually have more stringent conditions on how expressions can be formed.]

    Why use arrows in different directions in the two figures? Only because this is conventional. In the *flowchart* of Fig. 1.2 the right arrow expresses naturally the idea that a replaces b. But the notation in Algorithm 1.2 is more like that of computer programming languages in which the entity to be replaced almost always appears first. Programming languages use symbols

such as = or := instead of the left arrow but that is only because computer input devices (like the terminal at which this
page was typed) normally do not have the left arrow as a character.

3 The algorithms in Fig. 1.2 and Algorithm 1.2 both do precisely
the same task – adding 1 to I – but they are not quite literal
copies of each other. Do you see that the questions in Fig.
1.2 are asked slightly differently from the tests after **until** in
Algorithm 1.2?

Well, now, which of the figures do you like better? If this is your
first introduction to both these approaches, then we should expect
that you prefer Fig. 1.2 because its easy-to-follow pictorial qual-
ities make presentations by flowcharts congenial to many people.
Indeed, this kind of notation was widely used in the early days of
computers but is no longer used because it is quite unwieldy for
all but quite small algorithms. But that is not the only reason
we prefer the AL in Algorithm 1.2. We believe that, once you
get used to it, you'll find it easier to read and understand than
flowcharts. In particular, the notation in Algorithm 1.2 is much
more effective as a tool for reasoning about algorithms.

2 The properties of an algorithm

In order for a description of a computation to be valid, it must
have four properties:

- **Unique initialisation:** The action which starts off the algorithm must be unique.

- **Unique succession:** Each action in the algorithm must be
  followed by a unique successor action.

- **Finiteness:** That is, the application of the algorithm to a
  particular set of data (e.g. the values of A and B in Example
  1.1 or the value of I in Fig. 1.2 or Algorithm 1.2) must result
  in a finite sequence of actions.

- **Solution:** The algorithm must produce a solution to the
  problem it is intended to solve or it must indicate that, for

the given data, the problem cannot be solved by the algorithm. An example of the latter case would be an algorithm to solve quadratic equations which could only handle real numbers and could not, therefore, find the solution of a quadratic equation with complex roots. (Of course, it is possible to write an algorithm to solve quadratic equations which is not restricted to real numbers – see Section 1 of Chapter 4).

Usually it is the last of these properties which is the most difficult to establish. Hence the importance of the verification of algorithms mentioned earlier. Note that COUNTING has all the properties listed above.

■ Example 1.3: Multiplication

In this example we progress from counting to multiplication. Our purpose is to illustrate the ideas just presented and to provide yet another example of AL. Now we assume a slightly less rudimentary 'computer' than before, one that can perform ordinary addition but not multiplication so that we will have to instruct it to perform multiplication by doing repeated additions. Algorithm 1.3 is our multiplication algorithm.

Input x [Integer ≥ 0]
     y [Any integer]

Algorithm MULT

    $prod \leftarrow 0; u \leftarrow 0$ [Initialize $prod$ and u]
    repeat until $u = x$ [When $u = x$ skip rest of loop]
        $prod \leftarrow prod + y$
        $u \leftarrow u + 1$
    endrepeat

Output $prod$ [$= xy$]

Algorithm 1.3: Multiplication

This algorithm is even simpler than the one in Algorithm 1.2. To see just how it works, let's *trace*, that is, follow step-by-step, the algorithm as it tries to multiply $x = 5$ by $y = 13$. Here are the values of *prod* and u each time we enter the **repeat** ... **endrepeat** construct.

prod	0	13	26	39	52	65
u	0	1	2	3	4	5

On the next entry into the loop, after u has been set to 5, $u = x$ and execution of the algorithm is terminated.

This example illustrates various features of algorithms:

1 The **Input** must specify any constraints on the data (as, indeed, we did also in Algorithm 1.2). Do you see why we require x to be nonnegative but allow y to be any integer? What would happen if x were negative (Q1)? Which property of an algorithm listed in the previous section would fail to be satisfied in this case (Q2)? [At various places we shall ask questions in the text (numbered Q1, Q2 etc.) which will be answered at the end of the chapter.]

2 The **repeat** ... **endrepeat** construct or *loop*, which you've seen in both Examples 1.2 and 1.3, is a feature of essentially all significant algorithms. A general rule is this: If an algorithm does not have a series of steps which get executed again and again (i.e. a loop), then it probably does not perform any very worthwhile computation.

3 One feature of all loops is that there must be some way to emerge from the loop, that is, to stop executing it. For, if there were not, you would have an *infinite loop*, one which would go on for ever and so Property 3 of an algorithm would not be satisfied. Note that the test which allows you to stop executing the loop (such as $u = x$ in Algorithm MULT) does not assure that the loop will not be infinite. It just makes it possible that it won't be. Compare this paragraph with the answer to Q1 posed above.

4 Does Algorithm MULT satisfy Property 4 of an algorithm (Q3)? Even if we've convinced you that the output of the algorithm will always be the product of x and y, that isn't quite enough. It needs to be *proven* that the algorithm always works. We won't come back to this point again until Chapter 12 but you should keep it in mind as you read the rest of this book. We won't try to prove that the algorithms to be presented in Chapters 3 through 11 are correct because to do so would get pretty tedious. We shall, as here, only try to convince you of their correctness. You should keep in mind, however, that lurking behind our convincing arguments, there should be a proof somewhere.

SOME NOTES ABOUT THE REST OF THIS BOOK

1 Chapters 3 through 11 will teach you about algorithms by developing and discussing algorithms for a variety of tasks in mathematics and computer science, some familiar, some probably unfamiliar. In each case the algorithm will be developed and then there will be an exercise which asks you questions about the algorithm and related topics. Answers to the exercises are occasionally given immediately but, if not, they are always given in the answers-to-exercises section at the end of each chapter. We urge you to try to work the exercises before referring to the answers. A few sections, which we believe are quite difficult, are marked with an asterisk (*).

2 Many of the exercises are rather straightforward but some are quite difficult. Those in the latter category are marked with an asterisk before the problem number. When referring to one part of an exercise from within another part of the same exercise, we just give the part number in parentheses. For example, (3) in part 4 of Exercise 3.2 would refer to part 3 in that exercise. For references to a part of an exercise from outside that exercise, we use the exercise number followed by the part number in parentheses. Thus, 3.2(3) from anywhere outside Exercise 3.2 refers to part 3 of Exercise 3.2.

3 You don't have to read Chapters 3–11 in order so, if you wish, skip to an area of mathematics or computer science in which you are particularly interested. But be forewarned: aspects of AL and other notation and conventions will be introduced in various places and then used thereafter. So, if you skip ahead, you may find aspects of AL or other notation with which you are unfamiliar.

4 If you have a programmable calculator or a computer available to you, you will find it instructive to convert some of the algorithms we present to the language of your calculator or to some programming language (such as Pascal, whose features are very similar to those of our AL). In Chapter 13 we shall convert a few algorithms to computer and calculator programs.

5 Our AL uses **bold** text for the key words in algorithmic constructs. In addition, we use *italics* freely throughout the text to highlight important words and constructs.

6 Almost all the examples of computations we give use integers for the values of variables. This is for convenience only. Real numbers could have been used almost everywhere; integer examples are just easier to understand and manipulate.

■ ANSWERS TO QUESTIONS

Q1 The algorithm would never terminate because, since x is negative, u starts larger than x (at 0) and then gets larger still and so never equals x.

Q2 Finiteness because the algorithm would never terminate. In this case also, of course, the Solution property is not satisfied.

Q3 Yes, it does as we shall prove in Chapter 12.

2

Iterative and recursive algorithms

At the end of Chapter 1 we emphasized the importance of *loops*, that is, a series of steps that are executed repetitively, in any significant calculation. In this chapter we shall introduce the two main mechanisms for implementing repetitive calculations in algorithms. The first of these is *iteration* and the second is *recursion*. As we shall see, a recursive 'loop' is quite different in structure and intent from an iterative loop. In our discussion of iteration and recursion we shall introduce features of our algorithmic notation which will recur (pun intended!) again and again in this book.

1 Iteration

To *iterate* means to do repeatedly. Thus, in an algorithm, iteration is the repeated execution of some portion of the algorithm.

■ Example 2.1: Adding a list of numbers

First – as just about always in this book – we shall need some *mathematical* notation to enable us to specify and then solve the problem. Most, perhaps all, of the notation we shall use will be familiar to you; even when it is not, it should not cause you serious difficulties. (See Appendix 2 for a summary of the mathematical notation used in this book.) So, let's call our list of numbers A with the individual elements of the list denoted by

$$a_i, i = 1, 2, \ldots, n$$

with n denoting the number of elements in the list. Then an algorithmic construct for adding this list of numbers and putting the result in a variable called *sum* is

$$sum \leftarrow a_1$$
$$\textbf{for } i = 2 \textbf{ to } n$$
$$sum \leftarrow sum + a_i$$
$$\textbf{endfor}$$

Note several things about this algorithm fragment:

1 The *initialization* of *sum* to a_1 before the **for ... endfor** loop. Any time a variable like *sum* is used in an expression such as $sum + a_i$, it must first be given a value.

2 The use of the left arrow ($\leftarrow$), as in Chapter 1, to denote the *replacement* of one quantity *sum* by another $sum + a_i$. (In Chapter 3 we discuss the use of the left arrow more thoroughly.)

The loop above is called a *counter* loop because the effect of the *loop control* ($i = 1$ **to** n) is to *count* from 1 to n, adding a different element a_i each time. Many loops have this quality, but many others do not.

■ **Example 2.2: Largest power of 2 in N**

Here the problem is to find the positive integer n such that $2^n \leq N$ but also such that $2^{n+1} > N$. Here is an algorithm fragment to do this.

$$n \leftarrow 0$$
$$\textbf{repeat while } 2^{n+1} \leq N$$
$$n \leftarrow n + 1$$
$$\textbf{endrepeat}$$

Make sure you understand why this works and, in particular, why, after **while**, $n + 1$ is the correct exponent of 2. It may help to execute the algorithm for some small values of N.

Loops such as the one just above are sometimes called *decision* loops because their completion or *exit* depends upon a decision about whether an expression ($2^{n+1} \leq N$ above) is true or false.

(Expressions which can be true or false are called *Boolean expressions* after the English mathematician George Boole (1815–64) who first applied mathematics to logic.)

Loop constructs

We've relied on your intuition so far as regards your understanding of how loop constructs work. Here we'll list the loop constructs in AL that we've used thus far with a brief explanation of their *semantics* (i.e. meaning).

for $C = Cstart$ **to** $Cstop$ [**step** $Cstep$]
    S   [Any sequence of statements]
endfor

The sequence of statements S is executed repeatedly with the value of the *control variable* C set equal to $Cstart$ initially and then incremented by $Cstep$ at each new entry into the loop until C becomes greater than $Cstop$. The [. . .] implies that this part of the structure is optional. If it is absent $Cstep$ is implicitly +1. $Cstart$ and $Cstop$ can be variables or constants but they and $Cstep$ must all be integers. (What would happen if $Cstop > Cstart$ but $Cstep$ is negative? (Q1)) As an alternative to the above, **to** may be replaced by **downto** in which case $Cstart$ is decremented by the magnitude of $Cstep$ which, if absent, is implicitly −1. When **downto** is used, execution of the loop is terminated when C becomes less than $Cstop$.

repeat until Condition
    S   [Any sequence of statements]
endrepeat

Again the sequence of steps is executed repeatedly *until* the Condition (which must be a mathematical expression which is T(rue) or F(alse) depending upon the values of the variables in the expression) is T. If instead of **until** we have **while**, then S is executed *while* the Condition is T. For both **until** and **while** the test of the Condition is done at the *beginning* of the loop. Which one you use is a matter of personal preference. Although programming languages commonly use **while** at the beginning of a loop and **until** for a test at the end of a loop, we believe that, in thinking about the loop condition, it is often more natural to think in terms of *until* than *while* at the beginning of a loop. There is a form of the **repeat ... endrepeat** loop in which the test is made at the end of the loop. We'll introduce this in Chapter 3.

Loop constructs can be *nested*. Thus, one (or more) of the statements in S above may itself be a **repeat ... endrepeat** construct. You'll see examples of such nesting in later chapters.

■ **EXERCISE 2.1**

In each of the following write an algorithm fragment to carry out the following iterative tasks.

1 Repeat the task of Example 2.1 but don't use the **for ... endfor** construct.
2 Write an algorithm fragment to calculate the value of $n!(= n \cdot n - 1 \cdot n - 2 \cdots 2 \cdot 1)$ and put the result in a variable called *fact*.
3 Compute x^m when m is a positive power of 2 but don't just multiply x by itself m times. Put the result in a variable named *power*.
4 Now suppose m is not a power of 2. Use the fragment written in (3) and then complete the calculation of x^m.

2 Recursion

When you iterate, you do essentially the same calculation again and again until you are finished. Recursion is a quite different repetitive mechanism in which a calculation is performed, in effect, by jumping into the middle of it as if you knew how to do it and then somehow working your way out. If you've never encountered recursion before, this will seem quite strange and abstruse. In fact, although many people find recursion much harder to grasp than iteration, when you do understand it, you may find that not only is it a powerful style of reasoning but also a congenial one.

■ **Example 2.3: Adding a list of numbers recursively**

This is the same problem as in Example 2.1 but our solution is quite different. We suppose that – somehow – we know how to add a list of $n-1$ numbers and use this to add a list of n numbers:

$$\text{Sum}(a_i, i = 1, ..., n) = a_n + \text{Sum}(a_i, i = 1, ..., n-1)$$

But how do we sum a list of $n-1$ numbers? Well, we assume we know how to sum a list of $n-2$ numbers and add a_{n-1} to it. And so on working our way out (or 'down', if you like) until we have only one number to sum. But we know how to do that: it's the number itself. Now this may sound silly. Why are we making such a fuss about a problem for which we know a perfectly good solution – the one found in Example 2.1? Bear with us a while and you'll see that, at least from an algorithmic perspective, things are not quite as complicated as our description has been.

Here then is a recursive algorithm fragment to sum a list of numbers.

RecAddList(n)

> **if** $n = 1$ **then** $sum \leftarrow a_1$
> > **else** $sum \leftarrow sum + RecAddList(n-1)$
> **endif**

Note that the first line serves, in effect, to initialize sum which, as in Example 2.1, holds the sum of the numbers.

Even though we've hidden quite a bit of detail in the fragment above, perhaps you can see that this algorithm fragment does what our description above said it would – it calculates sum to be a_1 if the list has only one element and otherwise calculates it to be the sum of $n-1$ elements plus a_n. There are some other points worth noting about this algorithm fragment.

1 We gave the fragment a name – RECADDLIST (to suggest recursive addition of a list) – because in the fragment we had to refer to the name of the fragment. This aspect of *self-reference*, namely an algorithm referring to itself, is the essence of recursion.

2 We needed not only a name for the fragment but also a *parameter*, namely n. All recursive algorithms have a characteristic parameter, n in this example, such that the self-reference of the algorithm to itself always involves a *smaller* value of that parameter, $n-1$ in this example. This enables us to work our way out from n to a sufficiently small value of the parameter, 1 in this example, for which we know the answer. In this example, we know that the sum of one number is the number itself.

The decision construct

We have used **if** ...**then** ...**else** a few times already assuming that its meaning was intuitively clear. Now we'll be somewhat more formal. The general form of this construct is

> **if** Condition
> > **then** S1   [S1 is any sequence of statements]
> > [**else** S2]   [S2 is any sequence of statements]
>
> **endif**.

Its meaning is that, if the Condition is T, then the sequence of statements S1 after **then** is executed but if the Condition is F, the sequence S2, if it is present at all, is executed. If the **else** portion is absent then, if the Condition is F, the construct is said to be *empty* since nothing happens when the decision construct is executed.

If you haven't come across recursion previously, this one example will only serve as the barest – and perhaps not entirely comprehensible – introduction. And it certainly won't convince you that recursion is a competitor to iteration for repetitive calculations. But, when we return to recursion at various places later in this book (see Chapter 9, in particular), we hope you will not only find it quite understandable but will also see its value in solving problems on a computer.

■ EXERCISE 2.2

1 Write a recursive fragment to compute $n!$.

2 Write a recursive fragment to compute x^m.

3 This exercise is to test your ability to combine decision and iterative statements in a single algorithm. Given a list of integers $n_1, n_2, \ldots, n_m$ and another integer p, write an algorithm fragment to count the number of pairs $(n_i, n_j), i \neq j$ such that $n_i = p * n_j$ or $n_j = p * n_i$. (We shall use $*$ for multiplication since this is the symbol used in programming languages.)

■ ANSWER TO QUESTION

Q1 As $Cstep$ is negative, the control variable decreases at each step. But since $Cstop$ is larger than $Cstart$, C never becomes greater than $Cstop$ and so the loop never terminates.

■ ANSWERS TO EXERCISES

Exercise 2.1

1
```
sum ← 0
i ← 1
repeat while i ≤ n
    sum ← sum + a_i
    i ← i + 1
endrepeat
```

2
```
fact ← 1
i ← 2
repeat while i ≤ n
    fact ← fact * i
    i ← i + 1
endrepeat
```
calculate the value of $N! (= N \cdot N-1 \cdot N-2 \ldots 2 \cdot 1)$ & put the result in a variable called fact.

3
```
power ← x
count ← 1
repeat while count < m
    power ← power * power
    count ← 2 * count
endrepeat
```
compute x^m when m is a positive power of 2, but don't just multiply x by itself m times. put the result in a variable named power.

4
```
power ← x
count ← 1
repeat while 2 * count ≤ m
    power ← power * power
    count ← 2 * count
endrepeat
repeat while count < m
    power ← power * x
    count ← count + 1
endrepeat
```
suppose m is not a power of 2. use fragment written in 3. & then complete the calculation of x^m

If you don't see how this algorithm works, try it for two values of m, one a power of 2, one not.

Exercise 2.2

1 Factorial(n)

    if $n = 1$ **then** $fact \leftarrow 1$
             else $fact \leftarrow n * Factorial(n - 1)$
    endif

2 PowerOfx(m)

    if $m = 1$ **then** $power \leftarrow x$
             else $power \leftarrow x * PowerOfx(m - 1)$
    endif

Note that this solution is clearly inferior to our iterative solution to this problem since it does just what we told you not to do in Exercise 2.1, namely multiplying x by itself m times. A recursive fragment which follows the same general approach of our iterative fragment could be written but it would be a bit more complex than our solution here.

3 Here is a solution with the result put in a variable named *count*.

```
count ← 0
for i = 1 to m
    for j = i + 1 to m
        if n_i = p * n_j or n_j = p * n_i
            count ← count + 1
        endif
    endfor
endfor
```

Note the **or** in the condition after **if**. A condition with **or** is true if either the portion of the condition before **or** or after **or** is true or if both portions are true; the condition is false otherwise.

3
Number theory algorithms

In the remainder of this book you will learn about algorithms – how to design them and how to reason about them – by seeing and designing lots of algorithms yourself. We begin this chapter with four algorithms from the branch of mathematics called number theory. Three of them will address problems which are probably familiar to you; the fourth may well be unfamiliar but the problem itself is easily understandable.

1 Generating prime numbers

A prime number – or just a *prime* – is a positive integer > 1 which is divisible without remainder only by itself and 1. Thus, 2, 3, 5 and 7 are prime but 4 is not because it is divisible by 2 and 9 is not because it is divisible by 3. Our task here is to design an algorithm which generates the first N prime numbers where N is a positive integer. (Since the number of primes is infinite, N can be as large as you like.)

Before attempting to write any algorithm, you should think carefully about precisely what it is you want to do and how you are going to go about doing it. Here are some considerations to be taken account in designing an algorithm to generate prime numbers.

1 Since all primes except 2 are odd numbers, it will be sensible to treat 2 as a special case.
2 Our basic approach will be to test successive odd numbers to

see if they are prime by dividing them by odd numbers less than the number being tested. (This is not the most efficient approach – see below.)

3 But how do you test if one integer divides another? Remember that with an algorithm you must have some *procedure* which performs the desired test. We'll need a little mathematical notation. If i and j are integers, then

$$\lfloor i/j \rfloor$$

is the integer portion of the quotient. Another way of saying this is that $\lfloor i/j \rfloor$ is the largest integer not greater than i/j. Thus, $\lfloor 11/4 \rfloor = 2$, $\lfloor 9/13 \rfloor = 0$ and $\lfloor 36/6 \rfloor = 6$. The function defined in this way is called the *floor function*.

Then j divides i without remainder if and only if

$$\lfloor i/j \rfloor * j = i.$$

Do you see why this formula works (Q1)?

Algorithm 3.1 is our prime number algorithm. Since this is our first complete algorithm since the introductory examples in Chapter 1, a few comments are in order.

1 All algorithms in this book will have the **Input-Algorithm-Output** format with **Input** giving the data presented to the algorithm and **Output** giving the results of the algorithm. (In translating the algorithm to a computer program, the Input would have to be read in and the Output printed out.) Sometimes we shall include **print** statements in the algorithm when this is necessary (see Section 4 of this chapter) or when it will help make clear what the output is.

2 Note the right-justified comments. As you probably realized in earlier examples, these are intended to make the algorithm more understandable than just the algorithmic notation itself would be.

3 Near the end of the algorithm there is a line with two *statements* ($p_n \leftarrow i$ and $n \leftarrow n + 1$) separated by a semi-colon. Putting more than one statement on a line using the semi-colon as a separator is always permissible but should be done only when it will not interfere with readability.

4 Two aspects of the algorithmic notation should be mentioned:

Input N [Number of primes to compute]

Algorithm PRIMENUM

$p_1 \leftarrow 2$ [Label first prime p_1]
$n \leftarrow 2$ [n designates the prime p_n about to be calculated]
$i \leftarrow 3$ [First integer to test for primeness]
repeat until $n > N$
    $j \leftarrow 3$ [First test divisor]
    repeat until $j = i$ [If $j = i$ no divisor found]
        if $\lfloor i/j \rfloor * j = i$ **then exit** [Exit if i has divisor]
        $j \leftarrow j + 2$ [Try next divisor]
    endrepeat
    if $j = i$ **then** $p_n \leftarrow i; n \leftarrow n + 1$
[If $j = i$, then next prime found]
    endif
    $i \leftarrow i + 2$ [Next integer to be tested]
endrepeat

Output $p_n, n = 1, ..., N$

Algorithm 3.1: Prime numbers

- We've already considered the left arrow ($\leftarrow$) in Chapters 1 and 2. Stated somewhat more formally than previously, it has the meaning that the quantity on the right *replaces* the quantity on the left. A statement of the form *variable* $\leftarrow$ *expression* is called an *assignment statement* since it *assigns* the value of the expression to the variable.

- The **exit** means that the loop in which it is contained is exited. That is, it is not executed any further. When one loop is *nested* inside another, then only the innermost loop containing the **exit** is terminated.

Make sure you understand how this algorithm works. A good way to test that you understand any algorithm is to *hand trace* it. That is, choose a small value of N such as 5 and satisfy yourself that you see how the algorithm generates the first five prime numbers.

■ EXERCISE 3.1

1 Even with computers as fast as they are and getting faster, it is nevertheless important to make algorithms as efficient as possible. The efficiency of PRIMENUM depends upon the number of times $\lfloor i/j \rfloor$ needs to be calculated. (Do you see why (Q2)?) Calculate how many times this calculation must be performed for $N = 2, 4, 6, 8, 10$.

2 Actually PRIMENUM does a lot more calculation than is necessary. Can you work out how to change the condition on the inner **repeat** ... **endrepeat** loop so that much less computation needs to be performed?

3 When you exit the inner **repeat** ... **endrepeat** loop, you don't know whether the reason was that $\lfloor i/j \rfloor * j = i$ or that $j = i$. This is why the line after this loop is needed since this determines what the reason for the exit was. Instead of writing the loop this way, we could have written

> **repeat until** $j = i$ **or** $\lfloor i/j \rfloor * j = i$
> $\qquad j \leftarrow j + 2$
> **endrepeat**

Do you see why this works equally well (Q3)? Which way of doing this do you prefer? The answer is a matter of style, not science. It is very important to make your algorithms as readable as possible but readability is not a precisely defined concept.

2 *The greatest common divisor*

Euclid's algorithm to find the greatest common divisor (gcd) of two non-negative integers is the subject of this section. Let m and n be the two integers. Then the Euclidean algorithm to find the gcd of m and n, which we write as $\gcd(m, n)$, is based on the equation:

$$m = nq + r$$

where q is the integer quotient when m is divided by n and r is the integer remainder so that

$$q \geq 0 \quad \text{and} \quad 0 \leq r < n.$$

Thus, if $m = 315$ and $n = 91$, $q = 3$ and $r = 42$. It follows from the equation $m = nq + r$ that

$$\gcd(m, n) = \gcd(n, r)$$

because any number that divides m and n must also divide r and any number that divides n and r must also divide m. (We use 'divides' in the sense that one integer divides another if the quotient is an integer and there is no remainder. Thus, 7 divides 21 but not 23.) The equation above leads to the following sequence of equations where the roles of the numerator and denominator in one equation are assumed in the next equation by, respectively, the denominator and remainder in the previous equation.

$$
\begin{aligned}
m &= nq_1 + r_1 & 0 &\leq r_1 < n \\
n &= r_1 q_2 + r_2 & 0 &\leq r_2 < r_1 \\
r_1 &= r_2 q_3 + r_3 & 0 &\leq r_3 < r_2 \\
r_2 &= r_3 q_4 + r_4 & 0 &\leq r_4 < r_3 \\
&\;\;\vdots \\
r_{k-1} &= r_k q_{k+1} + r_{k+1} & 0 &\leq r_{k+1} < r_k \\
r_k &= r_{k+1} q_{k+2}.
\end{aligned}
$$

Since the sequence of remainders $r_1, r_2, \ldots, r_k, r_{k+1}$ is a decreasing sequence of non-negative integers, sooner or later one (r_{k+2} above) must be zero (why? – see the answer to Q4 on p. 32). Moreover, by the same argument as above, $\gcd(m, n) = \gcd(n, r_1) = \ldots = \gcd(r_k, r_{k+1})$. But $\gcd(r_k, r_{k+1}) = r_{k+1}$ since r_k is a multiple (q_{k+2}) of r_{k+1}. Therefore, $\gcd(m, n) = r_{k+1}$.

Algorithm 3.2 implements the sequence of equations above.

Comments:

1 Do you see how the loop in Algorithm 3.2 reproduces the sequence of equations above? It begins by initializing *denom* (for *denominator*) and *num* (for *numerator*) to m and n before the loop. Then each time through the loop the quotient (*quot*) and remainder (*rem*) are computed after which the old denominator becomes the new numerator and the remainder becomes the new denominator. Finally the loop is exited when the denominator becomes 0. Why must this happen at some stage (Hint: Why must each denominator be less than its predecessor (Q4)?)

Input m, n

Algorithm EUCLID

> $num \leftarrow m; \; denom \leftarrow n$
> **repeat until** $denom = 0$
> $\quad quot \leftarrow \lfloor num/denom \rfloor$ $\qquad$ [$\lfloor \ldots \rfloor$ is the floor function]
> $\quad rem \leftarrow num - quot * denom$
> $\quad num \leftarrow denom$
> $\quad denom \leftarrow rem$
> **endrepeat**

Output num

Algorithm 3.2: Greatest common divisor

---

2 *Initialization*, which we mentioned in Chapters 1 and 2, is almost always a feature of algorithms with loops. Before a loop is entered for the first time, the variables used within it must be given values.

3 Note the use of *mnemonic* variable names, as recommended in Chapter 1, which serve to suggest to you the roles served by variables. This will be a feature of all algorithms in this book and is a hallmark of any well-written algorithm. (There is a style – we might call it a literary style (don't laugh!) – which distinguishes a well-crafted algorithm from a pedestrian one.)

4 You have surely noticed by this time the careful indenting used in our algorithms. This, too, is a hallmark of a well-written algorithm as, indeed, is any feature which increases the readability of an algorithm.

■ EXERCISE 3.2

1 Apply EUCLID to $m = 315$, $n = 91$.

Answer

Just look at the following table of values for *num* and *denom*.

num	315	91	42	7
denom	91	42	7	0

so that $\gcd(315, 91) = 7$.

2 What would happen if instead we had $m = 91$, $n = 315$?

3 One way to check whether the gcd you have calculated is correct is to factorize m and n into their prime factors and calculate the product of the factors common to the two numbers. For example, $91 = 7 * 13$. Factorize 315 similarly to check that $\gcd(315, 91) = 7$.

4 We can also write loops in the form

> **repeat**
> $\vdots$
> **endrepeat when** *condition*

where the loop is exited *when* the condition after **when** is satisfied. Rewrite EUCLID using this form of a loop.

3 Least common multiple

The least common multiple (lcm) of two positive integers m and n is the smallest positive integer which is a multiple of them both.

■ EXERCISE 3.3

Show that $\gcd(m, n) * \text{lcm}(m, n) = m * n$.

Answer

The right idea is to express m and n in terms of their prime factorizations:

$$m = 2^{q_1} * 3^{q_2} * 5^{q_3} * \cdots$$
$$n = 2^{r_1} * 3^{r_2} * 5^{r_3} * \cdots$$

where the exponents q_i and r_i are non-negative integers. For example,

$$350 = 2 * 5^2 * 7 = 2^1 * 3^0 * 5^2 * 7^1$$

so that $q_1 = 1$, $q_2 = 0$, $q_3 = 2$ and $q_4 = 1$. Now suppose we denote by s_i the minimum of q_i and r_i and by t_i the maximum of q_i and r_i. Then

$$\gcd(m, n) = 2^{s_1} * 3^{s_2} * 5^{s_3} * \cdots$$

since each of the factors divides m and n and no greater number can divide them. Similarly

$$\text{lcm}(m, n) = 2^{t_1} * 3^{t_2} * 5^{t_3} * \cdots$$

since this is a multiple of both m and n and m and n cannot both be factors of any smaller number. Then, finally, since one of each of s_i and t_i is equal to q_i and the other is equal to r_i (do you see why (Q5)?)

$$q_i + r_i = s_i + t_i$$

from which the result follows.

Thus, to compute $\text{lcm}(m, n)$ it is enough to compute $\gcd(m, n)$ and then divide this into $m * n$. Algorithm 3.3 does this.

Notes:

1 For the first time we have invoked one algorithm (EUCLID) from within another (LCM). (We did, however, do essentially this in the recursive fragment in Section 2 of Chapter 2.) The first algorithm thereby becomes a *subalgorithm* called from within the *main algorithm*.

2 Refer to EUCLID to see that EUCLID places the value of the gcd into *num* which we then divide into $m * n$ to get the lcm.

Input m, n

Algorithm LCM

> EUCLID
> $lcm \leftarrow m * n / num$

Output lcm

Algorithm 3.3: Least common multiple

■ EXERCISE 3.4

1 Use LCM to calculate lcm(315, 91).

> **Answer** We found in Exercise 3.2 that gcd(315,91) = 7. There-fore, the *call* (i.e. the invocation) of EUCLID in LCD assigns 7 to *num* after which the next line calculates
>
> $$\text{lcm}(315, 91) = 315 * 91/7 = 4095.$$

2 Calculate lcm(6, 70) and lcm(35, 143) using LCM.
3 Check the answers to both calculations in (2) by using the prime factorisations of the numbers.

*4 Partitions of integers

A *partition* of a positive integer n is any set of positive integers which sum to n. Thus there are five partitions of 4:

$$
\begin{array}{cccc}
4 & & & \\
3 & 1 & & \\
2 & 2 & & \\
2 & 1 & 1 & \\
1 & 1 & 1 & 1
\end{array}
$$

Note that a partition is always written with the digits in non-increasing order.

Our problem is: given an integer n, generate all the partitions of n, beginning with n itself and continuing in *lexical order*, which refers generally to a systematic ordering (e.g. alphabetical or numerical) of a list. Two partitions are in lexical order if, beginning from the left, in the first digit in which the two partitions differ, the digit in the first one is greater than the digit in the second. Thus, the partitions of 4 above are in lexical order.

What we must determine then, given a partition P of n, is the next one in lexical order. There are two cases, one easy, one difficult:

Case 1: The last digit of P is not 1. Then just reduce this last digit by 1 and add a one at the end. For instance, from 2 2 above, we change the last 2 to a 1 and add a 1 to get 2 1 1.

Case 2: The last digit of P is 1. Then we must do the following:

(a) Starting from the right, count the number of 1s, call it c, until we finally get to a digit d greater than 1.

(b) Reduce d to $d-1$ which means that we still have $c+1$ to add at the end of the partition using digits no larger than $d-1$ (so that the digits of the partition will be in non-increasing order).

(c) Divide $c+1$ by $d-1$ to get an integer quotient q and remainder r. Then add q $(d-1)$s followed by one r (if $r > 0$) at the end.

Here's an example of Case 2 when $n = 25$ and the current partition is 8 6 4 1 1 1 1 1 1 1 . In this example $c = 7$ and $d = 4$. Dividing $(c+1)/(d-1) = 8/3$, we obtain $q = 2$ and $r = 2$. The next partition then is 8 6 3 3 3 2.

Algorithm 3.4 generates all the partitions of n. Note that i is called a *subscript pointer* because it designates the subscript of p.

Note the **print** statement. This is the first algorithm where the output had to be generated within the algorithm rather than just listed at the end. This is necessary since the calculation of each partition obliterates its predecessor.

Input n

Algorithm PARTITIONS

$p_1 \leftarrow n$	[First partition P is n]
$k \leftarrow 1$	[Length k of P is 1]
repeat	
print $p_m, m = 1, \ldots, k$	[Output current P]
if $p_k \neq 1$ **then**	[Is last digit 1 or not?]
$p_k \leftarrow p_k - 1$	
$p_{k+1} \leftarrow 1$	[Next P found]
$k \leftarrow k + 1$	[Increase value of k]
else	[$p_k = 1$]
$c \leftarrow 0; i \leftarrow k$	[Initializations; i is subscript pointer]
repeat while $p_i = 1$	[Find first digit $\neq 1$]
$c \leftarrow c + 1$	
$i \leftarrow i - 1$	[Move subscript pointer left]
endrepeat	
$p_i \leftarrow p_i - 1$	[$p_i = d$]
$q \leftarrow \lfloor (c+1)/p_i \rfloor$	[Integer quotient]
$r \leftarrow c + 1 - q * p_i$	[Integer remainder]
$j \leftarrow 1$	[Initialization]
repeat while $j \leq q$	[Fill in values of $d - 1$]
$p_{i+1} \leftarrow p_i$	
$i \leftarrow i + 1; j \leftarrow j + 1$	
endrepeat	
if $r = 0$ **then**	[Fill in last digit if $r \neq 0$]
$k \leftarrow i$	[Length of new P]
else	
$k \leftarrow i + 1$	
$p_k \leftarrow r$	
endif	
endif	
endrepeat when $p_1 = 1$	[All digits of P are 1]

Output All the partitions of n in lexical order

Algorithm 3.4: Partitions of an integer

■ EXERCISE 3.5

1 Hand trace PARTITIONS to generate all the partitions of 7. (Once you understand how PARTITIONS works, your 'hand trace' can just consist of writing down the partitions one after another.)

2 Explain how you would design an algorithm to generate the partitions in *reverse* lexical order (i.e. the digits in each partition should be in the same order as in PARTITIONS but the partitions themselves should be generated in the opposite order.

■ ANSWERS TO QUESTIONS

Q1 For any positive integers i and j we may write

$$\frac{i}{j} = \left\lfloor \frac{i}{j} \right\rfloor + \frac{r}{j}$$

where r is the integer remainder. Multiplying both sides by j:

$$i = j \left\lfloor \frac{i}{j} \right\rfloor + r$$

from which it follows that the formula in the text is correct if and only if $r = 0$.

Q2 The efficiency of any loop structure depends upon how often the innermost loop is executed. In PRIMENUM the floor calculation is the most significant item in the inner loop.

Q3 In PRIMENUM the loop is exited if $j = i$ or, immediately upon entering the loop, if $\lfloor i/j \rfloor * j = i$. This is precisely the same as asking, in the condition after **until**, if $j = i$ or $\lfloor i/j \rfloor * j = i$.

Q4 Since each remainder must be less than its predecessor, this means each value of *denom* is less than its predecessor since *denom* is replaced by *rem* in the loop. Since a strictly decreasing sequence (i.e. one in which each term is not just less than or equal to its predecessor but actually less) of non-negative numbers must, at some point, reach zero (why?), *denom* must sooner or later become 0.

Q5 If $q_i \neq r_i$, $\max(q_i, r_i)$ is one of s_i or t_i and $\min(q_i, r_i)$ is the other. If $q_i = r_i$, then $q_i = r_i = s_i = t_i$.

■ ANSWERS TO EXERCISES

Exercise 3.1

1 1, 6, 18, 36, 65
2 One simple change is not to consider any values of j greater than $\sqrt{i}$ since, if i has a factor greater than $\sqrt{i}$, it must also have a factor less than $\sqrt{i}$. So change the condition on the inner loop to **while** $j \leq \sqrt{i}$. Doing this, the answer to (1) would be 1, 3, 8, 13, 22.
3 We like the way it is done in PRIMENUM since the motivation for the two conditions is quite different. Therefore, it makes stylistic sense to put them in separate statements.

Exercise 3.2

2 The first pass through the loop would set $num = 315$ and $denom = 91$ and the rest would then proceed as before.
3 $315 = 3 * 3 * 5 * 7$. Since the only factor common to 91 and 315 is 7, this is the gcd.
4 The tricky point here is to avoid the division by zero when you first enter the loop if $n = 0$. So before **repeat** insert **if** $denom \neq 0$ **then** and end the loop with **endrepeat when** $denom = 0$.

Exercise 3.4

2 lcm(6,70) = 210; lcm(35,143) = 5005.
3 $6 = 2 * 3; 70 = 2 * 5 * 7$ so lcm(6,70) $= 2 * 3 * 5 * 7 = 210$.
$35 = 5 * 7; 143 = 11 * 13$ so lcm(35, 143) $= 5 * 7 * 11 * 13 = 5005$.

Exercise 3.5

1 The partitions of 7 are at the top of the next page.
2 Here are the rules to follow. Start with the partition of all 1s. Then:

- If the current partition ends in two or more 1s, just change the leftmost two 1s to 2.

```
7
6  1
5  2
5  1  1
4  3
4  2  1
4  1  1  1
3  3  1
3  2  2
3  2  1  1
3  1  1  1  1
2  2  2  1
2  2  1  1  1
2  1  1  1  1  1
1  1  1  1  1  1  1
```

- Otherwise the partition ends in a single 1 or a digit $\neq 1$.
  Work from right to left until you find the first digit less
  than the digit to its left (other than the rightmost digit
  itself) or the first digit of the partition if there is no digit
  less than the digit to its left. Increase the digit less than
  the digit to its left (or the first digit) by 1 and append a
  number of 1s equal to the sum of all of the digits to the
  right of the digit just increased, minus 1. For 44221 the
  first number less than the digit to its left is the first 2, so
  $44221 \rightarrow 44311$. Similarly $43332 \rightarrow 441111111$ and 4442
  $\rightarrow 5111111111$.

<u>4</u>
Algorithms from algebra

Even if you've forgotten a lot of the algebra you learned in secondary school, most of the problems we'll discuss in this chapter will seem familiar. But the algorithms we'll develop to solve them will have some features that you might not expect.

1 Solving quadratic equations

In this staple of elementary algebra you wish to solve

$$ax^2 + bx + c = 0$$

where a, b and c can be any real numbers. Even if you don't remember it, you'll probably recall that there is a formula, usually called the *quadratic formula*, to solve such an equation. It is

$$x = \frac{-b \pm \sqrt{b^2 - 4ac}}{2a}$$

where one solution of the quadratic equation is found using the $+$ sign before the square root and the other is found using the $-$ sign. You'll also remember that, since the quantity under the square root can be negative, the roots of the equation can be *complex numbers*. Nevertheless, an algorithm to solve quadratic equations should be straightforward. Just check the *discriminant* $b^2 - 4ac$ and do one thing if it is positive and another if it is negative and that should be it. Not quite. Our algorithm has two features you might not have thought of yourself:

1 In line with our previous dictum that a good algorithm must consider all possible cases, we make sure first that the equation really is quadratic, that is that $a \neq 0$. We also consider all other possible *degenerate* data.

2 When both roots are real, we use the quadratic formula to calculate just one of the roots and then calculate the other root in another way.

Algorithm 4.1 implements these notions.

This is much the longest algorithm we have presented so far. Make sure you follow its logic even if you don't understand the seemingly strange thing we have done to compute the real roots. Before we explain this, two notes about AL:

- In a **print** statement, an item in inverted commas is to be output just as it appears (but without the inverted commas). Such an item is called a *literal*.

- In two **print** statements there is a list of two elements separated by a comma. A list of items, separated by commas, is always allowable in a **print** statement.

Now we'll discuss the outstanding matters through an exercise.

■ EXERCISE 4.1

1 Any quadratic expression (where $a \neq 0$) can be factored in the form

$$a(x - x_1)(x - x_2)$$

where x_1 and x_2 are the two zeros which may be real or complex. Why is this so?

2 By multiplying out the form in (1), explain why the product of the two roots is always c/a. Note that we used this fact to compute the second real root in Algorithm 4.1.

3 When both roots are real, how do you know that the root computed by QUADEQN using the quadratic formula is the one of larger magnitude?

4 Consider the quadratic equation $x^2 + 10^{2n}x + 1 = 0$ where n is a positive integer. Using the quadratic formula to find both roots,

Input a, b, c

Algorithm QUADEQN

> **if** $a = 0$ [Not a true quadratic if $a = 0$]
>> **then if** $b = 0$ [Not even linear if $b = 0$]
>>> **then if** $c = 0$
>>>> **then print** 'Empty equation'
>>>> **else print** 'False equation'
>>>
>>> [The equation $c = 0$ is a contradiction if $c \neq 0$]
>>>> **endif**
>>>
>>> **else** $[b \neq 0]$
>>>> $x = -c/b$; **print** 'One real root:' x
>>>>
>>>> [Solution of linear equation $bx + c = 0$]
>>
>> **endif**
>
> **else** $[a \neq 0]$
>> $disc \leftarrow b^2 - 4ac$ [Calculate discriminant]
>> **if** $disc < 0$ **then**   [Complex roots]
>>> $real \leftarrow -b/2a$ [Real part of complex roots]
>>> $imag \leftarrow \sqrt{-disc}/2a$
>>>
>>>   [Imaginary part of complex roots]
>>> **print** 'Complex roots:' $real, imag$
>>>
>>>   [Actual roots are $real \pm i * imag$]
>>>> **else**   [Real roots]
>>> **if** $b \geq 0$ **then** $x1 \leftarrow (-b - \sqrt{(b^2 - 4ac)})/2a$
>>>
>>>   [Compute root of *larger* magnitude]
>>>> **else** $x1 \leftarrow (-b + \sqrt{(b^2 - 4ac)}/2a$
>>> **endif**
>>> $x2 \leftarrow c/x1 * a$ [Root of smaller magnitude]
>>> **print** 'Real roots:' $x1, x2$
>> **endif**
>
> **endif**

Output Two real roots *or* real and imaginary parts of complex roots *or* a single real root *or* an error message.

Algorithm 4.1: Quadratic equation

use your calculator to solve this equation for $n = 3, 4, \ldots$ until you find an n for which the root of smaller magnitude is given as 0 by the calculator. (It is easy to see that the true root cannot be zero.) Then for this value of n and again using your calculator, compute the two roots as in QUADEQN. How do you explain the two results using the two different approaches?

5 Use QUADEQN to find the roots of the following quadratic equations:

- $3x^2 - 5x + 8 = 0$
- $-4x^2 + 7x + 5 = 0$
- $2x^2 - 16x + 32 = 0$

2 Polynomial evaluation

A quadratic function (i.e. the left side of a quadratic equation) is just a special case of a *polynomial* for which the general form is

$$P_n(x) = a_n x^n + a_{n-1} x^{n-1} + a_{n-2} x^{n-2} + \cdots + a_2 x^2 + a_1 x + a_0$$

which we shall often write in the more compact form

$$P_n(x) = \sum_{i=0}^{n} a_i x^i.$$

If you aren't familiar with summation notation, then, as this example implies, it means that you take the quantity after the $\sum$ and evaluate it for each value of i implied by the limits above and below the $\sum$ and then add all the evaluated values together. Thus, for example,

$$\sum_{k=4}^{9} (2k + 3) = 11 + 13 + 15 + 17 + 19 + 21 = 96$$

$$\sum_{i=-2}^{2} i^{3i} = (-2)^{-6} + (-1)^{-3} + 0 + 1^3 + 2^6 = \frac{1}{64} - 1 + 1 + 64 = 64\frac{1}{64}$$

Given the coefficients $a_i, i = 1, \ldots, n$ and a value of x, here are three possible approaches to evaluating $P_n(x)$.

1 Evaluate $a_n x^n$, then evaluate $a_{n-1} x^{n-1}$, add it to the first term and then just continue evaluating terms and then adding them.
2 One clearly silly thing about the method described in (1) is that you evaluate x^n and then evaluate x^{n-1} again for the next step even though you probably already computed x^{n-1} on the way to evaluating x^n. So a better way is: evaluate $a_1 x$ and add it to a_0; then multiply x by itself to get x^2, save it and multiply it by a_2 and add $a_2 x^2$ to the sum already obtained. Then multiply x^2 by x to get x^3, save it and multiply it by a_3 and continue on in this way.
3 A still better way is to rewrite $P_n(x)$ as

$$P_n(x) = a_0 + x(a_1 + x(a_2 + x(a_3 + x(a_4 + \ldots x(a_n) \ldots)))).$$

Try a couple of values of n such as 4 and 5 to make sure you understand that this *nested* form of the polynomial is equivalent to the previous ways we have written it.

Algorithm 4.2 evaluates $P_n(x)$ using the third method above.

Input $n, a_0, a_1, \ldots, a_n, x$

Algorithm NESTEDEVAL

    $sum \leftarrow a_n$ [Initialize sum to a_n]
    for $k = n - 1$ **downto** 0
        $sum \leftarrow sum * x + a_k$
               [Multiply current sum by x and add next coefficient]
    endfor

Output sum

Algorithm 4.2: Nested evaluation of a polynomial

Note that we have used **downto** in a **for**-statement for the first
time here. The nested evaluation of a polynomial is often called
Horner's method after the English mathematician, William Horner,
1786–1837.

■ EXERCISE 4.2

1 For each of the three possible methods of evaluating a polynomial
listed above, calculate, as a function of n, how many multiplications and how many additions are required. What conclusions
do you draw?

2 Rewrite NESTEDEVAL using a **repeat** ... **endrepeat** loop instead of a **for** ... **endfor** loop.

3 Polynomial multiplication

One purpose of presenting this algorithm is to illustrate the idea
that a good way to test if you understand a piece of mathematics is
to try to design an algorithm to implement it. In secondary school
algebra you learned to perform calculations such as

$$(2x^3 - 4x^2 + 5)(-6x^2 + 3x + 4)$$

by multiplying each term in one polynomial by all the terms in the
other and then grouping together terms in the same power of x.
(What's the answer for the calculation above? (Q1)) Now we want
you to consider the general problem of polynomial multiplication:
Given two polynomials

$$P_n(x) = \sum_{i=0}^{n} a_i x^i$$

and

$$Q_m(x) = \sum_{i=0}^{m} b_i x^i,$$

what is their product? (In the example above $n = 3$ and $m = 2$.)
The hard part about this is figuring out how the phrase 'grouping
together terms in the same power of x' can be implemented in AL.
Think about this before you read Algorithm 4.3 for doing this. The
exercise after the algorithm should help you understand how the
algorithm works.

Input $n, a_0, a_1, \ldots, a_n; m, b_0, b_1, \ldots, b_m$

Algorithm POLYMULT

    for $k = 0$ **to** $m + n$
                [Range of powers in product is from 0 to $m + n$]
    $c_k \leftarrow 0; i \leftarrow 0; j \leftarrow k$
                [Initializations; c_k is coefficient in product]
    repeat while $i \leq n$ **and** $j \geq 0$
      if $j \leq m$ **then**
                [If $j > m$ there is no coefficient]
        $c_k \leftarrow c_k + a_i b_j$ [Add term to c_k]
      endif
      $i \leftarrow i + 1; j \leftarrow j - 1$ [New values of subscripts]
    endrepeat
    endfor

Output $c_k, k = 0, 1, \ldots, m + n$

Algorithm 4.3: Polynomial multiplication

This algorithm is short but quite tricky. The exercise should help
you to understand it. First, though, note two small additions to
our AL:

(a) the quantity after **to** or, for that matter, before **to** may be
an expression involving variables which must, of course, have been
given values in another statement or by being part of the Input;

(b) the **and** implies that the expressions before *and* after it must
be satisfied for the condition to be true.

■ **EXERCISE 4.3**

1 Hand trace POLYMULT to find the product of the two polynomials given at the beginning of this section.

2 Do the same for the following pairs of polynomials.

- $(x + 7)(-2x^5 + 3x^3 - 2x^2 + 7)$
- $(x^4 - 3x^3 - 2x^2 - 7x + 4)(-3x)$

3 Explain why the **if** statement is needed in POLYMULT.

*4 Actually the **if** statement isn't needed if you initialize i and j a little more carefully. Work out how to do this. (**Hint:** Express i as $\max(a, b)$; you have to figure out what a and b should be.)

*5 By this time you should understand how polynomial multiplication really works. As a final test that you do, complete the following equation

$$c_k = \sum_{i=max(0, k-m)}^{\cdots} a_{\ldots} b_{\ldots} \qquad k = 0, 1, \ldots, m + n$$

by filling in the upper limit of the sum and the two subscripts. Be careful! This is not easy.

4 Permutations

A permutation of n distinct objects taken k at a time is an arrangement of them in a row in which the *order* makes a difference. No object can be repeated. We shall denote the n objects by $1, 2, \ldots, n$. Thus, the following are the permutations of three objects, two at a time: 12, 13, 21, 23, 31, 32. The number of permutations of n objects, k at a time is denoted by $P(n, k)$. We'll focus here on the case $r = n$ in which the permutation consists of some ordering of all n objects.

Suppose we wish to generate a *random* permutation of n objects, r at a time. To do this we need a way to generate *random numbers* from the set $S = \{1, 2, \ldots, n\}$. Another feature of AL is that you may use mathematical functions in it at any place where you might have a variable in an expression. So we shall assume the existence of a function Rand$[1, n]$ which generates a member of S, with each choice equally likely, and such that the number generated on one call of Rand is independent of that generated on the previous call.

Input n

Algorithm PERMUTE

$Flag \leftarrow 0$ [Set all components of vector $Flag$ to 0]
for $i = 1$ **to** n
    repeat
        $r \leftarrow \text{Rand}[1, n]$ [Pick a random number]
    endrepeat when $Flag(r) = 0$
                                 [Until an unused one found]
    $Perm(i) \leftarrow r$ [ith member of permutation]
    $Flag(r) \leftarrow 1$ [Mark r used in $Flag$]
endfor

Output Perm   [The random permutation as a vector]

Algorithm 4.4: Random permutation

This use of functions in expressions in an algorithm is a special case of a more general AL facility discussed in the next section.

Algorithm 4.4 generates a random permutation. One note about the AL in this algorithm: *Flag* and *Perm* are both *vectors*, that is, ordered sequences of values. Sequences (see the next section) can be used freely in AL and their elements can be referred to using subscripts or, as here, indices in parentheses.

■ EXERCISE 4.4

1 You can't tell precisely how many random numbers must be generated in order to get all n distinct values needed for the permutation. But you can calculate the *expected number* of calls of Rand, that is, the average number of calls over many generations of a permutation of n objects. So suppose you have

generated j elements of the permutation. Why is $(n-j)/n$ the probability that a call of Rand will give you a value not yet in the permutation? Why, therefore, do you expect on the average to need $n/(n-j)$ calls of Rand to get the next element of the permutation? Use this result to express as a sum the expected (i.e. average) number of calls of Rand in the entire algorithm.

2 Display the elements of $P(3,3)$. Give a formula for $P(n,n)$.

3 It is unnecessary to go through the loop in PERMUTE n times because, after the $(n-1)$st time there is only one possibility for the nth item. Use this observation to modify PERMUTE so that the loop is executed only $n-1$ times.

4 PERMUTE is not very efficient. A more efficient idea is to set $Perm = 1, 2, \ldots, n$. Then, for $j = 1, 2, \ldots, n-1$, use $\text{Rand}(j, n)$ to generate a random number r in the set $j, j+1, \ldots, n$ followed by an interchange of the values of $Perm(j)$ and $Perm(r)$. Write an algorithm to do this and explain why this method works.

5 How many calls of Rand are needed for the algorithm you developed in (4)? How does this number compare with the sum you developed in (1) for $n = 8, 9, 10$. This comparison illustrates the value of thinking about a problem first (to get the algorithm in (4)) rather than just ploughing in as we did to get PERMUTE.

5 *The Fibonacci sequence*

A *sequence* is an ordered set of numbers, usually infinite, which can be written

$$a_0, a_1, a_2, a_3, \ldots$$

but we shall use the more common notation

$$\{a_n\}.$$

Sometimes the first term is denoted by a_1 instead of a_0.

One of the most famous sequences is the *Fibonacci sequence* $\{f_n\}$ which is most simply defined by the *difference equation*

$$f_n = f_{n-1} + f_{n-2}, \qquad f_0 = f_1 = 1.$$

Thus, each member of $\{f_n\}$, called a *Fibonacci number*, is the sum of the two previous members with the *initial conditions* to get you started being the given values of f_0 and f_1. Algorithm 4.5 is a recursive algorithm to generate the Nth Fibonacci number.

Input N [Assume ≥ 1]

Algorithm FIBONACCI

    function FIB(n)
        if $n = 0$ **or** $n = 1$
            then $Fib \leftarrow 1$ [Initial values]
            else $Fib \leftarrow$ FIB($n - 1$) + FIB($n - 2$) [From definition]
        endif
        return
    endfunc

    answer $\leftarrow$ FIB(N)

Output *answer* [$= f_N$]

Algorithm 4.5: The Fibonacci sequence

This is the first complete recursive algorithm we have presented. For the moment, don't try to understand it in fine detail but instead just see how the algorithm mirrors the definition of the Fibonacci sequence. But do note now the distinction between the name of the function (i.e. FIB) and the name of the variable (*Fib*), which must be the same as the name of the function and gives the value to be returned by the function to the calling algorithm. The point of the exercise below is to help you understand this algorithm in detail (but we had better admit now that there are some problems with it which we'll elucidate below).

First, however, there are some aspects of AL introduced in this algorithm which we need to discuss.

- A *function* is a separate piece of an algorithm (a *subalgorithm*) which is not necessarily recursive. It is invoked (called) from another algorithm by stating its name and its argument(s) and can appear anywhere in the calling algorithm where a variable would be appropriate in an expression. Thus, it cannot appear on the left end of an arrow ($\leftarrow$) which is why we have had to use the auxiliary variable *answer* above.

- Just as all our other structures have closing as well as opening keywords, so does a function, namely **endfunc**.

- Somewhere in the function its name without any arguments (i.e. *Fib* above) must appear as the left side of an assignment statement. It can, as above, appear more than once. The last value assigned to the function name is the value returned to the calling algorithm (i.e. Fibonacci itself above or Fib(n) if the call is recursive).

- The **return** statement, which need not be the last statement in the function, signifies the end of execution of the function and the return of control (i.e. execution) back to the calling algorithm.

■ EXERCISE 4.5

1 When $N = 3$ list all the calls of FIB(n) and the value each returns.

Answer

This is best explained by the table at the top of the next page where n is the value of the argument with which FIB is called and *Fib* is the value assigned before control is returned to the calling algorithm.

The *recursion level* measures how many calls of the function occurred before the evaluation of the function currently under way. Thus, FIB was first called from the algorithm itself with $n = 3$ and then from itself with $n = 2$ and then again from itself with $n = 1$. Note, in particular, that the value of f_1 is computed twice, once from the call of FIB($n-2$) when $n = 3$ and once from

n	Fib	Recursion level	Comment
3		1	First entry to FIB
2		2	Call of FIB$(n-1)$
1	1	3	Call of FIB$(n-1)$
0	1	3	Call of FIB$(n-2)$ with $n=2$ from level 2
2	2	2	Completion of level 2 call
1	1	2	Call of FIB$(n-2)$ from level 1
3	3	1	Completion of level 1 call

the call of FIB$(n-1)$ when $n=2$. This multiple computation of a single Fibonacci number is what we meant when we noted all was not quite well with FIBONACCI.

2 Can you use the result of (1) to indicate the calls of FIB and what is computed when $N=4$ and $N=5$?

*3 But what can you do to prevent the multiple computation of results? Here is one possibility. Use a vector F such that $F_i = 0, i = 0, 1, 2, \ldots N$ at the beginning of the algorithm but such that each time a value of f_i is computed, it is stored in this vector. Then, before calling FIB(n), you could check to see if f_n has already been computed. Modify FIBONACCI to implement this idea.

4 A still better idea is not to use a recursive algorithm at all. Rewrite FIBONACCI so that it computes the Nth Fibonacci number iteratively. (Perhaps this will just confirm to you that iteration is preferable to recursion. In Chapter 9 we'll try to convince you otherwise.)

6 Maximum and minimum of a set

Let $S = \{s_1, s_2, \ldots, s_n\}$ be a set of n elements where each element is a real number. We wish to find the maximum (or, alternatively, the minimum) number in the set. Algorithm 4.6 finds the maximum.

Input $n, s_1, s_2, \ldots, s_n$

Algorithm MaxNumber

$\quad m \leftarrow s_1$ [Set maximum (m) to first member of S]
$\quad$ **for** $i = 2$ **to** n
$\quad\quad$ **if** $s_i > m$ **then** $m \leftarrow s_i$ [Test s_i against m]
$\quad$ **endfor**

Output m [Maximum value]

Algorithm 4.6: Maximum of a set

One point should be noted about the AL in this algorithm. Note that the **if** statement is not concluded by an **endif**. We allow this when no ambiguity can result, particularly when the entire **if** statement is on a single line.

Our reason for presenting this algorithm is not because of any intrinsic interest in the algorithm itself – it is probably the simplest algorithm in this book – but rather to use it to illustrate some aspects of the analysis of algorithms.

■ **EXERCISE 4.6**

1 Show how you would modify MaxNumber to (a) find the minimum number in S; (b) find the maximum by first setting m to s_n and then proceeding down the list from s_{n-1} to s_1; (c) find the maximum and the second largest member of the set.

2 The only thing that changes in the application of MaxNumber from one set S to another is the number of times the assignment $m \leftarrow s_i$ in the **if** statement is executed. What is the *best case*, that is, the minimum number of times this assignment must be executed? Characterize the set S when this minimum is achieved.

3 What is the *worst case*, that is, the maximum number of times $m \leftarrow s_i$ may be executed? Characterize the set S in this case.

4 Determining the *average case*, that is, the average number of times $m \leftarrow s_i$ is executed is much harder. A useful simplification is to assume that all the s_i are distinct. Then we can assume with no loss of generality (why?) that the n members of the set are $1, 2, \ldots, n$. Now, for a given n, how many different orderings (i.e. permutations) are there of the n elements of the set?

*5 For $n = 2, 3, 4$, consider all possible orderings of $1, 2, \ldots, n$ and, for each ordering, determine how many times $m \leftarrow s_i$ in the **if** statement is executed. (It's a little tedious when $n = 4$ but do it anyway.) Then determine the average number of executions of $m \leftarrow s_i$ for each n. Can you make a conjecture of what the result is for any n? (**Hint:** Try to express the averages for $n = 2, 3, 4$ as the sum of quantities of the form $1/k$ where k is an integer.)

7 Bisection

A common problem in algebra is to find the root of an equation of the form

$$f(x) = 0.$$

Of course, the quadratic equation discussed at the beginning of this chapter is just such an equation. So, too, is $P_n(x) = 0$ when $P_n(x)$ is a polynomial of degree n. When $n = 3$ or 4 there are very tedious formulas analogous to the quadratic formula but for $n \geq 5$ there are no such formulas and, indeed, it can be proven that no such formulas can exist. So we need some other method to solve such polynomial equations. And when $f(x)$ is not a polynomial, $\tan x + \cos x$, for example, we need a *numerical* method to calculate the roots because there is no formula which will give the roots.

There are many methods available for solving $f(x) = 0$. In this section we present a simple but nevertheless very effective method called *bisection* which requires the assumption that $f(x)$ is a continuous function. It works as follows. Suppose, referring to Fig. 4.1, that we know two values of x, call them a and b, $a < b$, such that $f(x)$ is positive at one of them and negative at the other. Therefore, since $f(x)$ is continuous, there must be a root of $f(x) = 0$ between a and b. [To make things a bit simpler, we shall assume that there is precisely one root of $f(x)$ between a and b.] Then choose c to be

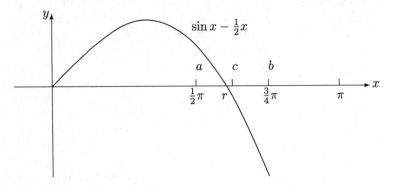

Figure 4.1: The bisection method. r is the root of $\sin x - \frac{1}{2}x = 0$.

the point half-way between a and b (so that it *bisects* the interval $[a, b]$). Then, unless we are very lucky and $f(c) = 0$, $f(c)$ will be either positive or negative and we will know that the root lies either in the interval $[a, c]$ or in $[c, b]$ (the former is the example shown in the figure). Now we just iterate, the result being that the interval in which we know the root lies is halved in size at each stage of the iteration. The result is a process which will find the true root only after an infinite number of steps but it typically very quickly finds an *approximation* to the root within whatever accuracy you desire.

Algorithm 4.7 implements this idea. Note the assumption in the input that what is input is not the function $f(x)$ itself but rather a subalgorithm to compute $f(x)$ such as was assumed with Rand in PERMUTE or such as we actually displayed in FIBONACCI. Note also that at each iteration $f(left)$ has the same sign as $f(a)$ and $f(right)$ has the same sign as $f(b)$.

■ EXERCISE 4.7

1. Show that $(left + right)/2$ is the midpoint of the interval $[left, right]$.
2. Why at the end do we compute $(left + right)/2$? So, when the algorithm terminates, how close must *root* be to the exact solution?

Input $f(x)$ [Really a procedure for computing $f(x)$]
    a, b [Such that $f(a)f(b) < 0$]
    ϵ [An error tolerance]

Algorithm BISECTION

    $left \leftarrow a; right \leftarrow b$ [Initialize left and right interval endpoints]
    repeat while $(right - left) > \epsilon$
        $x \leftarrow (left + right)/2$ [Midpoint of interval]
        if $f(x) = 0$ **then exit**   [Solution found]
            else
            if $f(x)f(a) < 0$ **then**
                $right \leftarrow x$ [$f(x), f(a)$ have different signs]
                     else
                $left \leftarrow x$ [$f(x), f(b)$ have different signs]
            endif
        endif
    endrepeat

    $root \leftarrow (left + right)/2$

Output *root*

Algorithm 4.7: Bisection

---

3 Use BISECTION to find a root of each of the following equations
with the given a and b and to within the tolerance ϵ given:

- $x^3 - 5x^2 - 17x + 21 = 0$, $a = 0, b = 3, \epsilon = 0.01$.
- $x^3 - 5x^2 - 17x + 21 = 0$, $a = -4, b = -1, \epsilon = 0.01$
- $\sin x - x/2 = 0$, $a = 1.5, b = 2, \epsilon = 0.01$

4 But suppose you are given an $f(x)$ but don't know values of
a and b such that $f(a)f(b) < 0$. Describe how you might find
suitable values of a and b. (You may assume that you know that
the root has magnitude less than some number M.) Implement
your idea in an algorithm.

■ ANSWER TO QUESTION

Q1 $-12x^5 + 30x^4 - 4x^3 - 46x^2 + 15x + 20.$

■ ANSWERS TO EXERCISES

Exercise 4.1

1 Any quadratic expression has two zeros. The expression in the statement of the exercise has the two zeros given and it has the same coefficient of x^2. Therefore, it must be the same expression.

2 Since the two expressions are the same, the product ax_1x_2 must be the same as c. Therefore, $x_1x_2 = c/a$.

3 In computing x_1 you ensure that it has the larger magnitude by using the negative square root when b is positive (so $-b$ is negative) and the positive square root when b is negative. Thus, $-b$ and the square root always have the same sign. Of course, if the square root is zero, then both roots are equal in magnitude.

4 On our calculator we get a root of 0 with $n = 5$ with the other root equal to 10^{10}. But using QUADEQN the small (in magnitude) root is 10^{-10}. This difference may seem too small to be important but there are calculations where accuracy to ten or more places is required.

5 First equation: complex roots - real part = 0.8333, imaginary part = 1.4044.
Second equation: 2.2947, -0.5447.
Third equation: equal roots of 4.

Exercise 4.2

1 Method 1: $\frac{1}{2}n(n+1)$ multiplications, n additions.
Method 2: $2n - 1$ multiplications, n additions.
Method 3: n multiplications, n additions.
Clearly Method 3 is the most efficient.

2 Replace the loop in NESTEDEVAL by

$$k \leftarrow n - 1$$
repeat
$$sum \leftarrow sum * x + a_k$$
$$k \leftarrow k - 1$$
endrepeat when $k = -1$

Exercise 4.3

1 For each k the table that follows gives each pair of values of i and j for which the value of c_k changes value, and the corresponding value of c_k.

k	i	j	c_k
0	0	0	20
1	0	1	15
2	0	2	−30
	2	0	−46
3	2	1	−12
	3	0	− 4
4	2	2	24
	3	1	30
5	3	2	−12

2 With tables as in the previous exercise,

For the first pair:

k	i	j	c_k
0	0	0	49
1	1	0	7
2	0	2	−14
3	0	3	21
	1	2	19
4	1	3	3
5	0	5	−14
6	1	5	− 2

For the second pair:

k	i	j	c_k
1	0	1	−12
2	1	1	21
3	2	1	6
4	3	1	9
5	4	1	−3

3 Without the **if** you might be using values of b_j which haven't been initialized and so the result would be rubbish.

4 Initialize as follows: $i \leftarrow \max(0, k - m), j \leftarrow k - i$ and then replace the **if** ... **endif** by just $c_k \leftarrow c_k + a_i b_j$.

5 Upper limit: $\min(k, n)$ and $a_i b_{k-i}$. Work this out for a few cases if you don't see why it is correct.

Exercise 4.4

1 The probability is $(n - j)/n$ because, from the n possibilities when Rand is called, only $n - j$ are successes. The average is $n/(n - j)$ because, when the success of a trial has probability p, on average it will take $1/p$ trials to get a success. (Think of a coin; it takes on average two tries to get a head.) The expected number of calls of Rand is $n \sum_{i=1}^{n}(1/i)$.

2 $P(3, 3)$: 123, 132, 213, 231, 312, 321; $P(n, n) = n!$.

3 Change n to $n - 1$ in the **for**-statement and at the end add

$$i \leftarrow 0$$
repeat
$\quad i \leftarrow i + 1$
endrepeat when $Flag(i) = 0$
$Perm(n) \leftarrow i$

4 Input n

Algorithm NEWPERMUTE

```
for i = 1 to n
    Perm(i) ← i                    [Initialisation]
endfor
for j = 1 to n − 1
    r ←Rand[j, n]
    Perm(j) ↔ Perm(r)             [Exchange j and r items]
endfor
```

Output *Perm*

This works because each pass through the second **for** loop causes a random element of those places of *Perm* not yet fixed (those from j to n) to be put in the jth position. Note that, after exit from the second loop, the element in $Perm(n)$ is the one you want there.

5 In NEWPERMUTE $n - 1$ calls of Rand are made for any n. In PERMUTE the average number of calls for $n = 8, 9, 10$ are, respectively, 21.74, 25.46, 29.29.

Exercise 4.5

2 For $n = 4$:

n	Fib	Recursion level	Comment
4		1	First entry to FIB
3		2	Call of Fib$(n - 1)$ from Level 1
2		3	Call of Fib$(n - 1)$ from Level 2
1	1	4	Call of Fib$(n - 1)$ from Level 3
0	1	4	Call of Fib$(n - 2)$ from Level 3
2	2	3	Completion of Level 3 call
1	1	3	Call of Fib$(n - 2)$ from Level 2
3	3	2	Completion of Level 2 call
2		2	Call of Fib$(n - 2)$ from Level 1
1	1	3	Call of Fib$(n - 1$ from Level 2
0	1	3	Call of Fib$(n - 2)$ from Level 2
2	2	2	Completion of Level 2 call
4	5	1	Completion of Level 1 call

For $n = 5$ we give only the values of n and, where it is given a value, Fib:

5; 4; 3; 2; 1, 1; 0, 1; 2, 2; 1, 1; 3, 3; 2; 1, 1; 0, 1; 2, 2; 4, 5; 3; 2; 1, 1; 0, 1; 2, 2; 1, 1; 3, 3; 5, 8.

3 Change the function FIB to:

```
function FIB(n)
    if F[n − 1] ≠ 0 then
        F[n] ← F[n − 1] + F[n − 2]   Values already calculated]
                    else
        F[n] ← FIB(n − 1) + F[n − 2]
```

[Value for $n - 1$ not yet calculated]

```
        endif
        Fib ← F[n]          [Value returned to calling algorithm]
        return
    endfunc
```

Note that the recursive call $\text{FIB}(n - 1)$ will result in $F[n - 2]$ being calculated at some point so that it will be known when needed. To initialize the array F add to the beginning of the main algorithm:

```
    F[0] ← 1; F[1] ← 1
    for j = 2 to n
        F[j] ← 0
    endfor
```

4 Input N

Algorithm FIBITER

```
    F_0 ← 1; F_1 ← 1
    for i = 2 to N
        F_i ← F_{i-1} + F_{i-2}
    endfor
```

Output F_N

Exercise 4.6

1 (a) Change $s_i > m$ to $s_i < m$; (b) Replace $m \leftarrow s_1$ with $m \leftarrow s_n$ and replace $i = 2$ **to** n with $i = n - 1$ **downto** 1;

(c) **Input** $n, s_1, s_2, \ldots, s_n$

Algorithm MAXTWO

```
    if s_1 > s_2 then
        m1 ← s_1; m2 ← s_2
            else
        m1 ← s_2; m2 ← s_1
```

```
    endif
    for i = 3 to n
      if s_i > m1 then
        m2 ← m1; m1 ← s_i
              else
        if s_i > m2 then
          m2 ← s_i
        endif
      endif
    endfor
```

Output $m1, m2$

2 Best case: no executions if s_1 is the maximum value.

3 Worst case: $n - 1$ executions if numbers are in ascending order.

4 $n!$. We can use $1, 2, \ldots, n$ because, since the number of permutations is $n!$ for any set of n distinct numbers, we might as well use the simplest set.

5 In each case we give the permutation followed by the number of executions of $m \leftarrow s_i$ in parentheses. For $n = 2$: 12(1), 21(0); the average is $1/2$. For $n = 3$: 123(2), 132(1), 213(1), 231(1), 312(0), 321(0); the average is $5/6$. For $n = 4$: 1234(3), 1243(2), 1324(2), 1342(2), 1423(1), 1432(1), 2134(2), 2143(1), 2314(2), 2341(2), 2413(1), 2431(1), 3124(1), 3142(1), 3214(1), 3241(1), 3412(1), 3421(1), 4123(0), 4132(0), 4213(0), 4231(0), 4312(0), 4321(0); the average is $26/24 = 13/12$. When $n = 2$, the average is $1/2$; for $n = 3$, the average is $5/6 = 1/2 + 1/3$; for $n = 4$ the average is $13/12 = 1/2 + 1/3 + 1/4$. The conjecture, which turns out to be correct, for the average for any n, therefore, is $\sum_{i=2}^{n} 1/i$.

Exercise 4.7

1 Since $(left + right)/2 - left = right - (left + right)/2 = (right - left)/2$, $(left + right)/2$ is the midpoint.

2 At the end $right - left < \epsilon$ so, by setting $root$ to the midpoint of the interval, we ensure an error of no more than $\epsilon/2$.

3 The midpoints of the successive intervals for the first equation are 1.5, 0.75, 1.125, 0.9375, 1.03125, 0.98348, 1.00781, 0.99609,

1.00195 which then gives a value for *root* of 0.99902.

The midpoints for the second equation are -2.5, -3.25, -2.875, -3.0625, -2.96875, -3.01562, -2.99219, -3.00391, -2.99805 and then $root = -3.00098$.

The midpoints for the third equation are 1.75, 1.875, 1.9375, 1.90625, 1.89062, 1.89844 and then $root = 1.89453$.

4 Input M

Algorithm FINDINTERVAL

```
    x ← 0                                        [Initialize]
    repeat while f(x) * f(x + 1) > 0 and x < M
        x ← x + 1                    [Search for positive crossing]
    endrepeat
    if x ≥ M then                    [No positive crossing found]
        x ← −1                                   [Initialize]
        repeat while f(x) * f(x + 1) > 0 and x > −M
            x ← x − 1                [Search for negative crossing]
        endrepeat
    endif
```

Output $x, x + 1$ [Crossing between x and $x + 1$]

Note than the $x > -M$ is not strictly needed since the assumption of the problem is that there is a root somewhere in the interval $-M < x < M$.

5
Searching and sorting

In the two preceding chapters we focused on algorithms for which the inspiration comes from mathematics. In this chapter we focus for the first time on algorithms from computer science. Searching and sorting are among the most basic applications of computers and are a staple of early university and even pre-university courses in computer science.

1 Sequential search

Much of the work computers do in administrative (as opposed to scientific or engineering) applications consists of looking things up in lists (such as the Inland Revenue's lists of taxpayers) and then doing some processing of the item found. But how do you find an item in a list which may have thousands or even millions of items on it? Sequential search is one answer.

We assume that the list we have is in lexical order (i.e. in alphabetical or numerical order) and that each item on the list has a *key* which is used when looking things up. This key might be a surname or a national insurance number (the latter type being preferable since national insurance numbers are (supposedly) unique whereas surnames are not). In any case we'll assume the keys are unique and that we are presented with a key to find in the list.

Three features of the AL in Algorithm 5.1, SEQSEARCH should be mentioned:

Input n [Number of items on list]
  $K_i, i = 1, 2, \ldots, n$ [List of keys]
  k [Key being sought]

Algorithm SEQSEARCH

  $i \leftarrow 1$ [Initialize index of position in list]
  repeat
    if $k = K_i$ **then print** i; **stop**   [Success]
      $k < K_i$ **then print** 'failure'; **stop**
      $k > K_i$ **then** $i \leftarrow i + 1$ [Try next key]
    endif
    if $i > n$ **then print** 'failure'; **stop**
  endrepeat

Output i [Index of key if found]
      or
    'failure'   [If key is not on list]

Algorithm 5.1: Sequential search

- The command **stop** ends execution of the algorithm. It is convenient to have this facility when the computation may be completed before all possible cases have been considered.

- This algorithm has a new **if** statement of the general form:

  if Cond1 **then** S1
    Cond2 **then** S2

        $\vdots$

    Condn **then** Sn
        [**else** S(n+1)]
  endif

  What do you suppose are the semantics (i.e. meaning) of this construct (Q1)?

- What does $k < K_i$ mean if the keys are words rather than numbers? Simply that this inequality is true if k precedes K_i alphabetically (or, more generally, lexically). Note that, since the keys are assumed to be in lexical order, once $k < K_i$, k cannot be equal to any subsequent K_i.

Note also the need for the 'failure' output. This is another example of the need to consider all possibilities, in this case that the key k being sought may not be on the list at all.

■ EXERCISE 5.1

1 Suppose the keys in the list are not in lexical order. Will SEQSEARCH still work? If not, how could it be changed so that it would work? It turns out that, for a list not in lexical order, sequential search is as efficient a method of searching as there is.
2 Explain why SEQSEARCH works, that is, why the sequence of three tests is correct.
3 How well this algorithm works depends upon the number of *comparisons* of k with some K_i. How many are there in the best case and the worst case?
4 Suppose we assume that k is a key on the list and that k is equally likely to be any K_i. On average, how many comparisons must be made? Before trying actually to calculate the answer, what does your intuition suggest to you that the average might be? If it turns out you are wrong, do you see why?

2 *Binary search*

You may recall the game in which someone picks a number between 1 and 100 and you try to guess it in the fewest tries. Each time you guess, you are told if you are correct, high or low. A good (actually, the best) strategy for this game if you wish, on average, to make the fewest guesses, is to guess 50 the first time and then to guess in the middle of each interval where you know the correct answer must lie. Algorithm 5.2, BINSEARCH implements this idea in searching for a key in an ordered list.

Input n

    $K_i, i = 1, 2, \ldots, n$

    k

Algorithm BINSEARCH

    $F \leftarrow 1; L \leftarrow n$ [Initialization of list pointers to
    repeat   first (F) and last (L) items]
        $i \leftarrow \lfloor (F + L)/2 \rfloor$ [Index of approximate midpoint]
        if $k = K_i$ **then print** i; **stop**   [Success]
          $k < K_i$ **then** $L \leftarrow i - 1$ [Search first half]
          $k > K_i$ **then** $F \leftarrow i + 1$ [Search second half]
        endif
        if $F > L$ **then print** 'failure'; **stop**
    endrepeat

Output i [Index of key if on list]

      or

    'failure'   [If key not on list]

Algorithm 5.2: Binary Search

Two remarks about this algorithm are appropriate:

1 The **if** before **endrepeat** does not have a closing **endif**. This is
allowed if no possible ambiguity can result.

2 There is no test at either end of the **repeat** … **endrepeat** loop.
This, too, is allowable if there is some construct within the loop
that will prevent the loop from being executed for ever. In this
case, the **stop**s within the loop ensure that execution of the loop
will terminate.

Ignore for the moment the test $F > L$ on the next to last line of
the algorithm. See if you understand how the rest of the algorithm
works. Figure 5.1 may help. It shows, for a particular list of keys,
how BINSEARCH would find the key being sought. You need to

understand how the successive comparisons of the search key with items in the list narrows the length of the list where the search key *might* be.

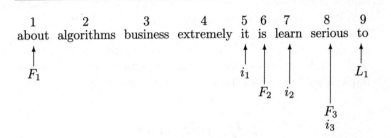

Figure 5.1: An example of binary search. Subscripts distinguish successive values of F, L and i. Let SERIOUS be the key being sought.

■ **EXERCISE 5.2**

1 Binary search bears some resemblance to how you look up a name in a telephone book. How is it similar to this process? How is it dissimilar?

2 Now look at the next to last line of BINSEARCH. Explain why $F > L$ – and only this – tells you that the key sought is not on the list.

3 How many comparisons of the search key with some K_i must be made in the best case of binary search?

4 For $n = 2, 3, \ldots, 10$ make a table of the number of comparisons which must be made in the worst case. (**Hints:** (a) Always consider the longest sublist that might have to be searched after a comparison of the (almost) middle object of the current sublist; (b) After the first comparison for each n, use the results already obtained for smaller values of n to determine the number of comparisons for the current value of n.) Using this table, can you make a conjecture about the worst case for binary search as a function of n?

5 Using the results for the worst case of sequential search and binary search, make a table comparing the two when the number of items on the list is $10^m, m = 1, 2, \ldots, 6$. What do you conclude about the relative efficiency of the two methods?

6 Binary search can also be implemented recursively. Write an algorithm fragment like those in Chapter 2 to do this. Your fragment should have two arguments, F and L, and should implement a binary search for a key k among the keys from K_F to K_L. Why do you think that, in fact, binary search is always implemented as in BINSEARCH and not recursively?

3 Bubble sort

In discussing sequential search and binary search we assumed that the lists we are searching are ordered. But how do we take an unordered list and make it ordered? This is the subject of *sorting*, one of the most widely studied areas of computer science.

Bubble sort is perhaps the simplest method of sorting, which is why we present it first. But – be warned – it is inefficient. In the next section and in Chapter 9 we shall present two better methods.

Suppose we are given an unordered list of n items, with keys $K_i, i = 1, 2, \ldots, n$, which we wish to sort in increasing (lexical) order of their keys. Imagine the keys are in a vertical list such as you might write on a piece of paper. Bubble sort works by comparing successive elements in the list and interchanging them if they are out of order so that small keys *bubble* to the top of the list and large keys sink to the bottom. Algorithm 5.3 implements bubble sort.

Note the nesting of the **for** loop inside the **repeat** loop. The efficiency of the algorithm will be determined by the number of times one key must be compared to another key in the inner loop. Exercise 5.3 below will explore this efficiency.

■ **EXERCISE 5.3**

1 Hand trace BUBBLE for the following list of nine items.

15 12 9 17 6 12 2 8 16

Input $n, K_i, i = 1, 2, \ldots, n$

Algorithm BUBBLE

> $i \leftarrow n - 1$ [Position of last comparison]
> **repeat**
>   **for** $j = 1$ **to** i
>   **if** $K_j > K_{j+1}$ **then** $K_j \leftrightarrow K_{j+1}$ [$\leftrightarrow$ denotes interchange]
>   **endfor**
> $i \leftarrow i - 1$
> **endrepeat when** $i = 0$

Output $K_1, K_2, \ldots, K_n$ [In lexical order]

Algorithm 5.3: Bubble sort

Note, in particular, what happens to the two 12s. Count the number of comparisons of one key with another and the number of times two keys are interchanged.

2 For each value of i, how many times is the inner loop executed? Use this result to express as a sum the total number of times the inner loop is executed. This sum should be familiar to you. What is its value as a function of n? When the efficiency of an algorithm as a function of its main parameter (n in this case) is a function of n^r ($r = 2$ in this case), we say that the algorithm is $O(n^r)$ (read 'order of n^r') which means that, for large n, when all smaller powers of n are insignificant compared to n^r, the efficiency can be very closely approximated by n^r times its coefficient in the expression for the efficiency ($1/2$ in this case).

3 Can you think of any ways to make BUBBLE more efficient? (There are some but even with them, bubble sort remains an $O(n^2)$ algorithm.)

4 The smallest possible number of interchanges is 0. What character must the list have for this minimum to be achieved?

5 What is the greatest possible number of interchanges as a function of n? What character must the list have for this maximum to be achieved?

4 Insertion sort

In this method of sorting we take the list of items to be sorted, one at a time, *inserting* each item in its proper place in the part of the list which has been sorted. Using the same list as in Exercise 5.3, we proceed as follows.

```
15
12 15
 9 12 15
 9 12 15 17
 6  9 12 15 17
 6  9 12 12 15 17
 2  6  9 12 12 15 17
 2  6  8  9 12 12 15 17
 2  6  8  9 12 12 15 16 17
```

Note how each time a new item is inserted, some other items have to be moved to the right (unless the new item is inserted at the end). Algorithm 5.4 implements this idea.

In the ith pass through the outer loop, keys K_1 to K_{i-1} are in order (although not generally in their final positions). (In the first pass only K_1 is in 'order'.) The algorithm starts at position $i - 1$ and works toward smaller subscripts until it finds the correct place to insert K_i. If j gets to 0, this means that K_i belongs at the beginning of the list (for now).

■ EXERCISE 5.4

1 The worst case of insertion sort occurs when, during each pass through the inner loop, you get to $j = 0$ before exiting. What must the order of the original list be for this to occur? In this case, how many comparisons of *temp* with K_j are made before the list is ordered?

2 So the worst case of insertion sort is as bad as bubble sort but remember that bubble sort is *always* this bad, irrespective of the order of the original list. How about the average case for INSERTION? This is harder but a plausible answer is obtained

Input $n, K_i, i = 1, 2, \ldots, n$

Algorithm INSERTION

> **for** $i = 2$ **to** n
> $temp \leftarrow K_i$ [Save ith key]
> $j \leftarrow i - 1$ [Determine where to insert ith key]
>   **repeat until** $j = 0$ **or** $temp \geq K_j$
>   [Final $j + 1$ is insertion point]
> $K_{j+1} \leftarrow K_j$ [Move keys to make room for K_i]
> $j \leftarrow j - 1$ [Work from end to beginning]
>   **endrepeat**
> $K_{j+1} \leftarrow temp$ [Insert K_i]
> **endfor**

Output $K_1, K_2, \ldots, K_n$ [In lexical order]

Algorithm 5.4: Insertion sort

---

by considering the average number of times the inner loop is executed. Why would you expect this to be $j/2$? Argue, therefore, that insertion sort is also $O(n^2)$ in the average case but that the coefficient of n^2 is $1/4$ rather than the $1/2$ for bubble sort.

3 Perform an insertion sort on each of the following lists.

- 8 5 12 21 1 9 2
- 4 9 11 17 13 21 3
- 18 24 22 9 5 11 3

In each case count the number of comparisons. Then for each list decide: is it more nearly an average case or a worst case?

In Chapter 9 we'll discuss a method of sorting which is better, on average, than insertion sort or bubble sort.

■ ANSWER TO QUESTION

Q1 In terms of **if-then-else** it means:

> **if** Cond1 **then** S1
> > **else if** Cond2 **then** S2
> >
> > $\vdots$
> >
> > > **else if** Condn **then** Sn
> > > > **else** S(n+1) [Only if present]
> > > > **endif**
> > >
> > > $\vdots$
> > >
> > > **endif**
> **endif**

■ ANSWERS TO EXERCISES

Exercise 5.1

1 It won't work as it is because k could be less than K_i even though the key sought is on the list. But it will work if you replace the first **if** statement by:

> **if** $k = K_i$ **then print** i; **stop**
> > **else** $i \leftarrow i + 1$
> **endif**

2 If the list items are in lexical order, then there are only three alternatives: (a) you've found the item you want, (b) you've passed the place it might be because it isn't there or (c) you haven't arrived yet where it might be.

3 Best case: 1; worst case: n.

4 Many people give the intuitive answer $n/2$ but the correct answer is $(n+1)/2$. Remember that half-way from 1 to 10 is not 5 but rather $5\frac{1}{2}$.

Exercise 5.2

1 It is similar in the sense that you normally open the book near where you think the entry might be; for many entries this means opening near the middle. And then, as with binary search, you go in the only direction possible. But it is dissimilar to binary search in that you never bisect precisely and, after the first try, you may guess pretty arbitrarily.

2 As you successively decrease the size of the sublist where the item may be, you will eventually get to a situation in which $F = L$ if the item is not present. At this point $F = L = i$. If the key you are looking for is not there, either $k < K_i$, in which case L is reduced by 1, and $F > L$, or $k > K_i$, in which case F is increased by 1, and again $F > L$. So either way, if the key is not present, you will get $F > L$.

3 1, if the first item looked at is the one sought.

4

n	2	3	4	5	6	7	8	9	10
Comparisons	2	2	3	3	3	3	4	4	4

For $n \geq 4$ you can find the correct number of comparisons c_n using the formula $c_n = c_{\lceil (n-1)/2 \rceil} + 1$. [The *ceiling* function ($\lceil \ldots \rceil$), analogous to the floor function introduced in Chapter 3, produces the smallest integer as large or larger than its argument. Thus, $\lceil (n-1)/2 \rceil$ equals $(n-1)/2$ if n is odd and equals $n/2$ if n is even.)] The given formula works because, after the first comparison (which gives rise to the +1 in the formula), the *longer* sublist remaining to be searched has length $\lceil (n-1)/2 \rceil$.

The worst case number of comparisons for binary search for general n is $\lfloor \log_2 n \rfloor + 1$. [The logarithm L to the base 2 of a quantity q is such that $2^L = q$. Thus, $\log_2 4 = 2$ and $\log_2 32 = 5$.]

5 The table which follows makes clear the greater efficiency of binary search.

Length of List	Worst case number of comparisons for:	
	Sequential search	Binary search
10	10	4
100	100	7
1000	1000	10
10000	10000	13
100000	100000	16
1000000	1000000	19

Clearly binary search is much more efficient than sequential
search for all but quite short lists.

6 Here is the fragment which we call BinSearchRec(F, L).

>   **if** $F > L$ **then print** 'failure'
>   **else**
> $i \leftarrow \lfloor (F + L)/2 \rfloor$
>   **if** $k = K_i$ **then print** i; **stop**
> $k < K_i$ **then** BinSearchRec($F, i - 1$)
> $k > K_i$ **then** BinSearchRec($i + 1, L$)
>   **endif**
>   **endif**

Binary search is always implemented iteratively because the iterative version is just as simple to write as the recursive one and,
in addition, it executes faster because recursion requires a level
of computer overhead not necessary for iteration.

Exercise 5.3

1 Starting from the list 15 12 9 17 6 12 2 8 16, we get:

Pass number				List					
1	12	9	15	6	12	2	8	16	17
2	9	12	6	12	2	8	15	16	17
3	9	6	12	2	8	12	15	16	17
4	6	9	2	8	12	12	15	16	17
5	6	2	8	9	12	12	15	16	17
6	2	6	8	9	12	12	15	16	17

Number of comparisons: $8 + 7 + 6 + \cdots + 1 = 36$. [Note that
there is a Pass 7 (with one comparison) because, even though
the list is sorted after Pass 6, the computer doesn't recognize
this.]

Number of interchanges: $7 + 5 + 3 + 3 + 2 + 1 = 21$

2 For each value of i the inner loop is executed i times. Therefore,
the total number of executions of the inner loop is
$1 + 2 + 3 + \cdots + n - 1 = n(n - 1)/2$.

3 (i) You could record if an interchange has been made on a given
pass through the list. If not, the list is in order and you can

stop; (ii) Keep track of where the last interchange takes place on each pass and, on the next pass, only compare up to that point because all subsequent items are already in their final positions; for an algorithm which implements this idea see the answer to 12.2(3).

4 The list must be already in order.

5 When the list is in reverse order, there are $n(n-1)/2$ interchanges, the same number as there are comparisons.

Exercise 5.4

1 The worst case is when the numbers are originally in descending order in which case the number of comparisons is $1 + 2 + \cdots + (n-1) = n(n-1)/2$.

2 The number of passes through the inner loop can be anything from 0 to j so the average is $(j+0)/2 = j/2$. Since, as i goes from 2 to n, the starting value of j goes from 1 to $n-1$, the sum of the averages is $[1 + 2 + \cdots + (n-1)]/2 = n(n-1)/4$ with the coefficient of n^2 equal to $1/4$.

3 The number of comparisons is, respectively, 14, 11, 18. For a list of length 7, the expected number of comparisons is $7 \times 6/4 = 10.5$ so the first two are not too far from the average but the last one is pretty bad, not surprisingly since it is close to being in reverse order.

6
Algorithms from linear algebra

Linear algebra deals broadly with those problems in algebra that have their origins in matrix algebra and the solution of linear equations and linear inequalities. It is one of the most important branches of mathematics because so much of the rest of the mathematical edifice depends upon it. In addition, it is one of the most useful branches of mathematics. The three algorithms in this chapter are examples of the use of algorithms in matrix algebra and the solution of linear equations. For the latter, which constitutes perhaps the single most widespread use of computers in mathematics, we give two contrasting algorithms.

1 Matrix multiplication

A *matrix* is a rectangular array of numbers

$$\begin{bmatrix} a_{11} & a_{12} & \cdots & a_{1n} \\ a_{21} & a_{22} & \cdots & a_{2n} \\ \vdots & \vdots & & \vdots \\ a_{m1} & a_{m2} & \cdots & a_{mn} \end{bmatrix}$$

where the first subscript identifies the row number $(1, \ldots, m)$ and the second denotes the column number $(1, \ldots, n)$. We shall often use a single upper-case letter, such as A, to denote the entire matrix and occasionally we shall denote the entire matrix by $[a_{ij}]$. *Matrix algebra* is concerned with adding, subtracting and multiplying two matrices $A = [a_{ij}]$ and $B = [b_{ij}]$. Adding and subtracting are defined only when both matrices have the same numbers of rows and columns and have the (almost) obvious definitions (but what are these (Q1)?). Multiplication AB of two matrices, A and B, however, is trickier and is defined only when the number of columns of A is the same as the number of rows of B. (When two matrices satisfy this property, they are called *conformable*.) If this is the case, then we call the product matrix $C = [c_{ij}]$ and let A be $m \times k$ (that is, A has m rows and k columns) and B be $k \times n$. Then the element c_{ij} in the ith row and jth column of C is defined as

$$c_{ij} = \sum_{r=1}^{k} a_{ir} b_{rj}$$

which means that c_{ij} is found by taking the ith row of A and multiplying each element of this row by the corresponding term in the jth column of B (why are the numbers of elements in the ith row of A and the jth column of B the same (Q2)?) and then adding all these products together. This row-by-column multiplication is often called an *inner product*.

Once you understand the definition of the product matrix C, Algorithm 6.1 to compute C almost writes itself. This is the only triply-nested algorithm you will see in this book. (Recall the discussion of nesting in Section 1 of Chapter 2.) You need to realize that the deeper the nesting, the more computation must be done in each pass through the outer loop. We shall explore this a bit further in the exercise which follows.

■ EXERCISE 6.1

1 Do a hand trace of MATRIXMULT for the following pair of matrices.

$$A = \begin{bmatrix} 2 & -5 & 3 \\ -3 & 4 & -2 \\ 0 & -3 & 1 \end{bmatrix} \qquad B = \begin{bmatrix} -5 & 0 & 2 \\ -3 & 4 & 2 \\ 3 & 6 & -1 \end{bmatrix}$$

2 Suppose A is $m \times k$ and B is $k \times n$. How many multiplications and how many additions are performed while executing MATRIXMULT?

Input m, k, n, A, B [Dimensions and elements of A and B]

Algorithm MATRIXMULT

    for $i = 1$ **to** m
      for $j = 1$ **to** n
        $c_{ij} \leftarrow 0$ [Initialize c_{ij}]
        for $r = 1$ **to** k
          $c_{ij} \leftarrow c_{ij} + a_{ir}b_{rj}$ [Compute inner product]
        endfor
      endfor
    endfor

Output C [The mn elements of the product matrix]

Algorithm 6.1: Matrix multiplication

---

3 When A and B are *square*, that is, when they have the same number of rows as columns, state the condition on their dimensions so that they will be conformable. What is the answer to (2) when A and B are square?

4 For very large matrices (with, say, dimensions over 1000) matrix multiplication can take a long time even on very fast computers, so it is desirable to make an algorithm like MATRIXMULT as efficient as possible. One time-consuming aspect of MATRIXMULT is finding where in the computer's memory the quantities with particular subscripts are located. Try to reformulate MATRIX-MULT so that, instead of having c_{ij} appear three times in the algorithm, it only appears once when its final value is assigned to it.

5 Write separate algorithms for matrix addition and subtraction. Can you see how to do this in a single algorithm by adding to the input a quantity which indicates whether you are adding or subtracting? Replacing more than one algorithm by a single algorithm not only saves memory but can be a useful way to see explicitly a common relation among algorithms.

2 Gaussian elimination

In secondary school you certainly solved simultaneous linear systems of two equations in two unknowns of the following form.

$$\begin{aligned} 4x - 7y &= 5 \\ 2x + y &= 7. \end{aligned}$$

In this section we'll consider the solution of n linear equations in n unknowns which, using the notation developed in the previous section, we express as

$$\begin{aligned} a_{11}x_1 + a_{12}x_2 + \cdots + a_{nn}x_n &= d_1 \\ a_{21}x_1 + a_{22}x_2 + \cdots + a_{2n}x_n &= d_2 \\ \vdots \qquad\qquad \vdots \qquad\quad \vdots \\ a_{n1}x_1 + a_{n2}x_2 + \cdots + a_{nn}x_n &= d_n. \end{aligned}$$

A convenient notation for this system is $A\mathbf{x} = \mathbf{d}$ where A is a matrix and $\mathbf{x}$ and $\mathbf{d}$ are *vectors*. In this notation a vector is just an $n \times 1$ matrix and so matrix multiplication, as defined above, gives the system of equations above.

A method you probably learned for solving a system of two equations was to *eliminate* one of the variables. Thus, in the example above, if we multiply the first equation by $1/2$ and subtract it from the second equation, x is eliminated and we are left with

$$\frac{9}{2}y = \frac{9}{2}$$

from which we get $y = 1$. Substituting this back in the first equation, we get $x = 3$. *Gaussian elimination* is just a generalization of this idea to any number of equations.

- Eliminate x_1 from each equation except the first by multiplying the first equation by suitable constants and then subtracting it from each of the other equations.

- Then eliminate x_2 from each equation except the first *two* by multiplying the second equation by suitable constants and subtracting it from all the rest (except the first).

- Continue in this way to eliminate x_i from the $(i+1)$st to the nth equation for $i = 3, 4, \ldots, n-1$ to obtain finally

$$
\begin{array}{rcl}
a_{11}^* x_1 \; + \; a_{12}^* x_2 \; + \; a_{13}^* x_3 \; + \; \cdots \; + \; a_{1n}^* x_n & = & d_1^* \\
a_{22}^* x_2 \; + \; a_{23}^* x_3 \; + \; \cdots \; + \; a_{2n}^* x_n & = & d_2^* \\
a_{33}^* x_3 \; + \; \cdots \; + \; a_{3n}^* x_n & = & d_3^* \\
\vdots & & \vdots \\
a_{nn}^* x_n & = & d_n^*
\end{array}
$$

  where the asterisks (*) indicate that the coefficients in the system after elimination are generally different from those in the original system. (In the first row, the coefficients are the same as in the original system but we have added asterisks to them, too, for uniformity and to simplify what follows.)

- Now working from the bottom up, the value of each unknown may be calculated. From the last equation $x_{nn} = d_n^*/a_{nn}^*$. Then

$$
x_{n-1} = (d_{n-1}^* - a_{n-1,n}^* x_n)/a_{n-1,n-1}^*
$$

  and, in general

$$
x_i = \left(d_i^* - \sum_{j=i+1}^{n} a_{ij}^* x_j \right)/a_{ii}^*.
$$

  This bottom-up calculation of the values of **x** is called the *back substitution*.

It is not hard to turn this procedure into Algorithm 6.2.

Input $n, A, \mathbf{d}$

Algorithm GaussElim

> **for** $i = 1$ **to** $n - 1$ [Elimination loop]
> > **for** $k = i + 1$ **to** n
> > [Subtract multiple of equation i from equations $i + 1$ to n]
> > > $m \leftarrow a_{ki}/a_{ii}$ [Multiple to be subtracted]
> > > $a_{ki} \leftarrow 0$ [Element which becomes 0]
> > > **for** $j = i + 1$ **to** n
> > > > $a_{kj} \leftarrow a_{kj} - ma_{ij}$ [New values for row k]
> > >
> > > **endfor**
> > > $d_k \leftarrow d_k - md_i$
> >
> > **endfor**
>
> **endfor**
> **for** $i = n$ **downto** 1 [The back substitution]
> > **for** $j = i + 1$ **to** n
> > > $d_i \leftarrow d_i - a_{ij}x_j$ [Subtract known terms]
> >
> > **endfor**
> > $x_i \leftarrow d_i/a_{ii}$ [Solution value]
>
> **endfor**

Output x   [Values of solution vector]

Algorithm 6.2: Gaussian elimination

■ **EXERCISE 6.2**

1 Do a hand trace of GaussElim for this system of equations.

$$3x_1 + 4x_2 - 3x_3 = 3$$
$$2x_1 - 2x_2 + 4x_3 = 12$$
$$-3x_1 + x_2 + 4x_3 = 16$$

2 Does GaussElim always work? No, it doesn't. What can cause it to fail? (**Hint:** Which of the four arithmetic operations sometimes is impossible to carry out?)

3 One simplification of GAUSSELIM occurs when, instead of calling the vector of right-hand sides **d**, you just denote d_i by $a_{i,n+1}$. Rewrite GAUSSELIM with this simplification.

*4 Go back to (1) and count the number of (a) multiplications, (b) additions and subtractions and (c) divisions you performed. (Include additions, subtractions and multiplications by 0 because, of course, in general these coefficients wouldn't be zero.) Then go to GAUSSELIM and try to make the same count as a function of the number of equations n. Leave the answers in the form of sums if you wish.

3 The Gauss-Seidel method

In this section we present a second algorithm for the same task as in the previous section, namely, solving simultaneous linear equations. Why should we want to do this? After all, Gaussian elimination is an effective way to solve such equations. If you completed (4) of Exercise 6.2 or studied the answer at the end of the chapter, you will know that the number of multiplications [which affects how fast the algorithm executes more significantly than additions and subtractions (which are faster) or divisions (of which there are many fewer)] is approximately $n^3/3$. Since modern, fast computers can do millions of multiplications each second, this should be fast enough, shouldn't it? Generally, yes, but computers have now solved simultaneous equations when $n > 100\,000$. When $n = 100\,000$, $n^3/3$ is $10^{15}/3$ so that, even if your computer can do 10 million multiplications a second, it will take about $10^8/3$ seconds which is almost $10\,000$ hours. So there is motivation to look for a faster method than Gaussian elimination. The method we shall discuss in this section is *sometimes* faster than Gaussian elimination.

This method is an *iterative* method called the Gauss-Seidel method. By iterative we mean that we perform a sequence of essentially identical steps, each time getting a solution which is closer to the true solution than at the previous step. How many steps do we need until we find, as Gaussian elimination does, the true solution? In fact, the Gauss-Seidel method *converges*, that is achieves the true solution, only after an infinite number of steps. But what good is that? And how could it possibly be faster than Gaussian elimination if it requires an infinite number of steps? Good questions! – which we'll answer later. For now, bear with us and try to believe that what we shall do will not be a waste of time. (It won't be.)

The basis of the Gauss-Seidel method is to assume a solution $\mathbf{x} = (x_1, x_2, \ldots, x_n)$ of a system of n equations and then try to compute a better solution which we'll call $\mathbf{y} = (y_1, y_2, \ldots, y_n)$. Here's how we'll do this. Using the notation of the previous section, we compute y_1 as follows.

$$y_1 = -\left(\frac{1}{a_{11}}\right)\left(\sum_{j=2}^{n} a_{1j}x_j - d_1\right).$$

What we have done here is solve for x_1 in the first equation and then use the assumed values $x_2, x_3, \ldots, x_n$ to compute y_1. Similarly, solving for x_2 in the second equation and then using $x_3, x_4, \ldots, x_n$ as well as the just-computed y_1, we compute y_2 as

$$y_2 = -\left(\frac{1}{a_{22}}\right)\left(a_{21}y_1 + \sum_{j=3}^{n} a_{2j}x_j - d_2\right).$$

In general, then, y_k is computed using the just-computed $y_1, y_2, \ldots, y_{k-1}$ and the assumed values $x_{k+1}, x_{k+2}, \ldots, x_n$ as

$$y_k = -\left(\frac{1}{a_{kk}}\right)\left(\sum_{j=1}^{k-1} a_{kj}y_j + \sum_{j=k+1}^{n} a_{kj}x_j - d_k\right)$$

for all other k from 3 to n. Then having done this, we turn right around and let the just-computed values of $\mathbf{y}$ become the assumed values of $\mathbf{x}$ and repeat the process all over again. If we're lucky – more on that below – successive values of $\mathbf{y}$ will get closer and closer to the true solution.

But when do we stop? We can't continue this process for ever so we must stop when we think that the last computed value of $\mathbf{y}$ is close enough to the true solution. We do this by comparing two successive values of $\mathbf{y}$ (really by comparing $\mathbf{y}$ with the $\mathbf{x}$ used to compute it – why is this sufficient (Q3)?). We stop when the two

are close enough to each other on the assumption – some danger
here (see below) – that if two successive values of **y** are near each
other, then they are both near the true solution. (Compare this
notion of *convergence* with that used to halt BISECTION in Chapter
4.)

Algorithm 6.3 implements this method which is called the *Gauss-Seidel iteration.*

Input $n, A, \mathbf{d}$
$\qquad \epsilon$ $\qquad\qquad\qquad\qquad$ [Tolerance used to decide when to stop]

Algorithm GAUSSSEIDEL

$\quad$ **repeat**
$\qquad$ $diff \leftarrow 0$ $\qquad\qquad$ [Initialize difference between **y** and **x**]
$\qquad$ **for** $k = 1$ **to** n
$\qquad\quad$ $y_k \leftarrow -(1/a_{kk})(\sum_{j=1}^{k-1} a_{kj}y_j + \sum_{j=k+1}^{n} a_{kj}x_j - d_k)$
$\qquad\quad$ $diff \leftarrow diff + (x_k - y_k)^2$
$\qquad\quad$ [Update sum of squares of difference between **x** and **y**]
$\qquad$ **endfor**
$\qquad$ **for** $i = 1$ **to** n $\quad x_i \leftarrow y_i$ $\quad$ [**y** becomes **x** for next iteration]
$\quad$ **endrepeat when** $diff < \epsilon$

Output x $\qquad\qquad\qquad\qquad$ [Last computed value of solution]

Algorithm 6.3: The Gauss-Seidel method

Now this algorithm should raise a number of questions, not least
of which, perhaps, is why would you ever want to use it when safe,
reliable GAUSSELIM is available. We'll consider some of the other
questions in the exercise below but let's answer this one now. First,
it's not true that GAUSSELIM does find the true solution of $A\mathbf{x} = \mathbf{d}$.
Oh, yes, it would if we could carry out all the arithmetic with perfect accuracy but we can't because the elements of A and $\mathbf{d}$ are
typically expressible only by infinite decimals. Entering them into
a computer inevitably involves a *roundoff* error. Moreover, each

arithmetic operation typically involves another roundoff when the result is expressed in a form that can be accommodated in a computer memory. The stringing together of all these roundoffs can sometimes create enormous errors so that the result of applying GAUSSELIM may not be close to the true solution at all. Roundoff is typically a smaller problem with GAUSSSEIDEL because, no matter how many iterations you do, you start each iteration with the original coefficient matrix so the roundoff errors can only build up separately during each iteration. So, in cases where roundoff is a problem with GAUSSELIM, GAUSSSEIDEL has the potential to be more accurate. Indeed, variations of GAUSSSEIDEL, designed to make it even more accurate and more rapidly convergent, are those used most often in solving very large systems of linear equations on computers.

So how about the questions we asked near the beginning of this section? First, how can the Gauss-Seidel method be a good one when it requires an infinite number of steps to converge? You've probably already seen the answer to this. It is that, on the one hand, you can get as accurate solution as you wish by setting ϵ as small as you wish in GAUSSSEIDEL and, on the other, GAUSSELIM seems to get the exact answer but doesn't really because of roundoff error. Second, how fast is GAUSSSEIDEL compared to GAUSSELIM? In (4) of Exercise 6.2 you showed that the number of operations performed in executing GAUSSELIM is about $\frac{1}{3}n^3$. From the **for**-loop in GAUSSSEIDEL you can see fairly easily that each iteration requires about n^2 operations. Thus, roughly speaking $n/3$ Gauss-Seidel iterations require about the same amount of computation as GAUSSELIM. Not only are $n/3$ iterations often enough to get the accuracy you wish but, in addition, for coefficient matrices with many zeros – which is common in the solution of very large systems – GAUSSSEIDEL can be modified to take advantage of this but GAUSSELIM cannot. So, in fact, for reasons of both speed and accuracy, GAUSSSEIDEL can be a very sound alternative to GAUSSELIM.

Before getting to the exercise, we should mention one thing about the use of AL in GAUSSSEIDEL. The second **for** statement has no matching **endfor**. As with **if** statements, we allow this when the entire statement fits on one line and no ambiguity from omitting the **endfor** is possible.

■ EXERCISE 6.3

1 Hand trace GAUSSSEIDEL for the following system.

$$
\begin{aligned}
4x_1 - x_2 &= 2 \\
- x_1 + 4x_2 - x_3 &= 6 \\
- x_2 + 4x_3 &= 2.
\end{aligned}
$$

As a starting vector **x** choose $x_1 = x_2 = x_3 = 0$ and let $\epsilon = 0.01$. It should be clear from your last **x** what the solution is converging to. Check that these values actually do solve the system. (It's worth noting that GAUSSSEIDEL is most effective and, indeed, generally does converge for *diagonally dominant* systems, that is systems like this one where the diagonal coefficients are the largest ones. Note also that the two zero coefficients make the computation easier at each iteration. On the other hand, zero coefficients at the beginning do not remain zero after the first stage of GAUSSELIM.

2 In GAUSSSEIDEL the main statement in the loop has two summations in it. We wrote it this way so that GAUSSSEIDEL could easily be related to the equations above. But we could have calculated y_k entirely in AL by converting the sums into **for** loops. Do this.

3 GAUSSSEIDEL compares **y** to **x** by computing the sum of the squares of the difference of corresponding components of the two vectors. Why do it this way? Why not instead just compute the sum of the magnitude of the differences (i.e. the absolute value of the differences)?

4 We presented separate equations for y_1, y_2 and another separate one for the other y_k but used only one equation for all y_i in GAUSSSEIDEL. Why does this work all right?

5 Did you notice that the initial value of x_1 is never used in any equation? Does this mean that x_1 in the initial assumed solution could be any value?

6 Suppose that the output statement in GAUSSSEIDEL had been **Output y**. Would this have been all right? Why?

■ ANSWERS TO QUESTIONS

Q1 With $C = A \pm B$ the element of the sum is given by $c_{ij} = a_{ij} + b_{ij}$ and the element of the difference by $c_{ij} = a_{ij} - b_{ij}$.

Q2 For two conformable matrices the number of columns of the first (and, thus, the number of elements in each row) is the same as the number of rows of the second (which is the number of elements in each column).

Q3 Because the **y** used at the previous stage is the **x** with which the current **y** is compared.

■ ANSWERS TO EXERCISES

Exercise 6.1

1 The result is

$$\begin{bmatrix} 14 & -2 & -9 \\ -3 & 4 & 4 \\ 12 & -6 & -7 \end{bmatrix}$$

2 For each element of the product there are k multiplications and $k - 1$ additions. So the total for the mn elements is mnk multiplications and $mn(k - 1)$ additions.

3 Two conformable square matrices must both be $n \times n$. The number of multiplications in multiplying two such matrices is n^3 and the number of additions is $n^2(n - 1) = n^3 - n^2$.

4 Replace $c_{ij} \leftarrow 0$ with $temp \leftarrow 0$ and replace the statement in the inner **for** loop by $temp \leftarrow temp + a_{ir}b_{rj}$ and then, after the first **endfor** insert $c_{ij} \leftarrow temp$.

5 Here is the algorithm for combined addition and subtraction:

Input m, n, A, B
       g   [=0 for addition, 1 for subtraction]

Algorithm MATRIXADDSUB

    for $i = 1$ **to** m
        for $j = 1$ **to** n
            $c_{ij} \leftarrow 0$ [Initialization]

```
        endfor
    endfor
    for i = 1 to m
        for j = 1 to n
            c_{ij} ← a_{ij} + (−1)^g b_{ij}
        endfor
    endfor
```

Output C $[= [c_{ij}]]$

Exercise 6.2

1 The first of the following tables gives the relevant values during the elimination stage and the second table gives the values during the back substitution.

i	k	m	a_{k1}	a_{k2}	a_{k3}	d_k
1	2	0.6667	0	−4.6667	6	10
	3	−1	0	5	6	19
2	3	−1.0714	0	0	7.4286	29.7143

i	d_i	x_i
3		4
2	−14	3
1	3	1

2 An attempt to divide by zero (i.e. $m = 0$) at any stage causes GaussElim to fail.

3 In the input eliminate **d** (and note that the input of A assumes that A has n rows and $n + 1$ columns, the last column being **d**). In the inner elimination loop, change $j = i + 1$ **to** n to $j = i + 1$ **to** $n + 1$ and eliminate the d_k statement at the end of this loop. In the back substitution loop, change d_i everywhere to $a_{i,n+1}$.

4 For the system in (1): eleven multiplications, eleven additions/subtractions and six divisions. In general for an $n \times n$ system the number of multiplications and additions is the same. In the inner loop of the elimination, this is $n - i + 1$. But this inner loop is executed $n - i$ times for each i. Thus, the total is $\sum_{i=1}^{n-1}(n - i)(n - i + 1)$ (which can be shown to be $(n^3 - n)/3$). For the back substitution loop the number of multiplications in the inner loop is $n - i$ so the total is $\sum_{i=1}^{n}(n - i)$ which is $n(n - 1)/2$. Thus, the total number of multiplications and additions is $(n^3 - n)/3 + n(n - 1)/2 = \frac{1}{6}(2n^3 + 3n^2 - 5n)$. The number of divisions is $\sum_{i=1}^{n-1}(n - i) = n(n - 1)/2$ from the elimination loop and n from the back substitution for a total of $n(n + 1)/2$.

Exercise 6.3

1 The first three iterations are as follows:

x_1	x_2	x_3
0.5	1.625	0.90625
0.90625	1.953125	0.98828125
0.98828125	1.994140625	0.99853515625

As you can see, these are converging to $x_1 = 1, x_2 = 2, x_3 = 1$ which do, indeed, solve the system.

2 Here is the rewritten **for**-loop.

> **for** $k = 1$ **to** n
> $\quad c \leftarrow 0; f \leftarrow 0$ $\qquad\qquad\qquad\qquad$ [Initialize]
> $\quad$ **for** $j = 1$ **to** $k - 1$
> $\quad\quad c \leftarrow c + a_{kj}y_j$
> $\quad$ **endfor**
> $\quad$ **for** $j = k + 1$ **to** n
> $\quad\quad f \leftarrow f + a_{kj}x_j$
> $\quad$ **endfor**
> $\quad y_k \leftarrow (1/a_{kk}) * (c + f - d_k)$
> $\quad diff \leftarrow diff + (x_k - y_k)^2$
> **endfor**

3 You could use the sum of the absolute value of the differences but the sum of squares is more commonly used in mathematics because the square is an *analytic* function (i.e. in particular, it can be differentiated) while the absolute value is not (i.e. it has no derivative at the origin).

4 Because the first sum in y_k in the algorithm is empty when $k = 1$ and gives the correct single term when $k = 2$.

5 Yes; the value given to x_1 initially is never used in the algorithm.

6 It would be all right because the last thing done in the algorithm (in the last line of the loop) is to set **y** to **x**.

7
Graph and tree algorithms

The algorithms we'll discuss in this chapter are members of a class of algorithms that are very important in computer science because they are applicable to many areas of science and engineering.

A *graph* is not the beast you may remember from secondary school – or that you may be familiar with if you use a graphics calculator – which is a picture of a function. In combinatorial mathematics a graph is a structure, such as that shown in Fig. 7.1 (overleaf), which consists of a set of points called *vertices* and a set of lines called *edges*. The edges, such as those shown in Fig. 7.1, may be *undirected*, in which case we just call it a graph, or they may be directed in which case we speak of a *digraph*. Later in this chapter we'll discuss a particular and very important kind of graph called a *tree*.

1 The adjacency matrix

If you wish to design an algorithm for a task based on graphs, you immediately face a problem we have been able to ignore so far in this book because, for all the algorithms we have considered, the resolution of this problem was transparently clear. This problem is the *representation* problem: how do you represent in an algorithm (or a computer program) the *data structures* with which the algorithm must deal? For graphs, one solution to this problem would be to use a list of edges of the graph, each edge being represented by the two vertices at its ends. This is satisfactory in some circumstances but, for large graphs with many edges, finding the edge you want on such a list can be very unwieldy. The algorithm we are about to present uses another representation which is both more effective and more elegant for many graph applications.

The problem we wish to address is whether or not there is a *path*, that is a sequence of edges, which leads from one vertex to another and, if so, how long that path is (i.e. how many edges there are on the path). In a digraph the edges must be traversed in the directions of their arrows but in a graph they may be traversed in either direction. If two vertices of a graph or digraph are joined by an edge, they are said to be *adjacent*. Our tool for solving this problem is the *adjacency matrix* of a graph which is an $n \times n$ array, where n is the number of vertices in the graph. With the vertices numbered from 1 to n as in Fig. 7.1, the element of the adjacency matrix in the ith row and jth column of this matrix is 1 if vertex i is adjacent to vertex j and 0 if it is not. In a digraph the 'from' and 'to' are interpreted literally but in a graph, if there is a 1 in the (i, j) position, there is also a 1 in the (j, i) position so that the adjacency matrix is *symmetric*.

The adjacency matrix for the graph of Fig. 7.1 is as follows.

$$
\begin{bmatrix}
0 & 1 & 0 & 1 & 0 & 0 \\
1 & 0 & 1 & 1 & 1 & 0 \\
0 & 1 & 0 & 0 & 0 & 1 \\
1 & 1 & 0 & 0 & 0 & 0 \\
0 & 1 & 0 & 0 & 0 & 1 \\
0 & 0 & 1 & 0 & 1 & 0
\end{bmatrix}
$$

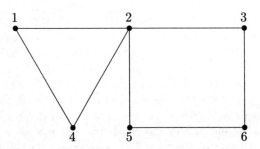

Figure 7.1: An example of a graph

Our algorithm is based on a theorem that we state without proof. Let A denote the adjacency matrix of a graph. Then in the matrix A^m (the mth power of A; recall the description of the product of two matrices in Chapter 6), the element in row i and column j consists of the number of paths of length m from vertex i to vertex j. (Note that the adjacency matrix itself represents all the paths of length 1, namely the edges.)

Using MATRIXMULT from Chapter 6, we then have Algorithm 7.1 to find the number of paths of length m between all pairs of vertices in a graph or digraph.

Input A [Adjacency matrix of graph]
      m [Length of paths desired]

Algorithm PATHNUMBER

     $B \leftarrow A$ $[B$ holds $A^k]$
     for $k = 2$ **to** m
         MATRIXMULT(A, B, C) [Using MATRIXMULT from Ch. 6]
         if $k < m$ **then** $B \leftarrow C$ $[A^k$ from C to $B]$
     endfor

Output C $[= A^m]$

Algorithm 7.1: Number of paths in a graph

There are several noteworthy things about this very short, simple algorithm.

1 The first line of the algorithm is an assignment statement which replaces *all* the values of one matrix by those of another. Our AL allows such matrix operations (and even matrix algebra) without restriction except, of course, that the dimensions of the two matrices must conform.

2 Not only have we used a previous algorithm (MATRIXMULT) as a subalgorithm but we have given it *arguments* $(A, B$ and $C)$ with A and B the two matrices to be multiplied and C the result matrix so that $C = AB$. The arguments enable us to use MATRIXMULT as a subalgorithm in any other algorithm whatever the names of the matrices in those algorithms. Note also the implicit assumption that the dimensions of both matrices are known when they are named, although this could be made explicit by adding arguments for the dimensions of A and B (both $n \times n$ in this case). If you are converting some of our algorithms to programs for a hand-held calculator, you may not be allowed to call subprograms with arguments but you can probably finesse this problem by using the same matrix names in the program and subprogram.

3 Note that, after the first iteration of the **for** loop (with $k = 2$), $C = AB = A^2$ which then replaces B. After the next iteration, $C = AB = A\, A^2 = A^3$ and so on until $C = A^m$ at the end of the loop.

■ **EXERCISE 7.1**

1 Execute PATHNUMBER with $m = 3$ for the adjacency matrix given just before the algorithm.

2 Use Fig. 7.1 to list all the paths of length 3 between the following pairs of vertices – $(1, 4)$ and $(3, 6)$ – and confirm that the number of such paths agrees with the result of (1).

2 Depth first search

Think now of a graph as a structure in which, at each vertex, some information is stored. For example, the graph might represent the kinship relationships among members of some community, with the vertices representing people and an edge between two vertices meaning that a relationship exists between the two people. The information stored at each vertex might be some important data about the person associated with that vertex. Suppose then we want to search the graph to collect some group statistics (e.g. the

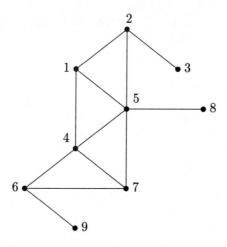

Figure 7.2: A sample graph for depth first search.

distribution of ages). We would start at some vertex and move from vertex to vertex, updating whatever statistics we were collecting.

But how could we be sure that we had *visited* every vertex (i.e. processed the information at each vertex) and how could we arrange never to revisit any vertex? (This would be easy in a graph of the size of Fig. 7.2 but how about a graph with several hundred or more vertices and edges?) The algorithm of this section presents a method which will visit each vertex of a graph once and only once if the graph is *connected*, that is, if there is at least one path between each pair of vertices.

The idea of *depth first search* is to start at an arbitrary vertex and go from vertex to vertex, marking each one as it is visited, until either you have visited all vertices or you can't proceed any further without going to a vertex already visited. If this happens, we *backtrack* along the path (but not visiting the vertices again, that is, not processing the data at vertices already visited) until we arrive at a vertex connected to an unvisited vertex, after which we again proceed as far as we can, backtrack, if necessary, etc. Do you see from our description that depth first search is naturally recursive (Q1)? Algorithm 7.2 implements depth first search.

Input G [A graph in some representation]

Algorithm DEPTHFIRSTSEARCH

    procedure DEPTH(u)   [u is a vertex]
      Visit u [Process information at vertex u]
      Mark u 'visited'   [So we don't visit u again]
      for w in $A(u)$ [$A(u)$ is the set of vertices adjacent to u]
        if w is not marked 'visited' **then**
            DEPTH(w)   [Recursive call]
      endfor
      return   [When all adjacent vertices visited]
    endpro

    Mark all vertices 'not visited'   [Main algorithm; initialize]
    Choose a vertex v arbitrarily
    DEPTH(v)   [First call of DEPTH]

Output Results of processing information at each vertex

Algorithm 7.2: Depth first search

Several novel aspects of AL are used in DEPTHFIRSTSEARCH.

- A **procedure** is another kind of subalgorithm. Unlike a function it does not need to be called in an expression, nor does it have to compute a single value as a function does. Otherwise its structure and use are directly analogous to that of a **function**. If you are familiar with a programming language such as Pascal, you will recognize the parallel between subalgorithms in AL and subprograms in a programming language.

- The portion of the algorithm following DEPTH is explicitly called the 'main algorithm'. This is common terminology to distinguish the portion of an algorithm which calls a subalgorithm from the subalgorithm itself.

- More than in any previous algorithm we have used plain English ('Choose a vertex v arbitrarily'). This is always acceptable in an algorithm when the alternative in formal AL would not serve a useful purpose and, indeed, might only serve to confuse by making the algorithm unnecessarily complex. Of course, plain English does not convert to a programming language as easily as the formal parts of AL but, whenever the choice is between readability (of an algorithm) and convertability (to a computer program), we choose the former.

- Note that we do not specify the representation of the graph G as a list of edges or as an adjacency matrix. Although representation is a crucial issue which justified the presentation of PATHNUMBER, we do not specify a representation when that is unnecessary in order to understand an algorithm.

■ EXERCISE 7.2

1 By hand tracing DEPTHFIRSTSEARCH show the order in which the vertices of Fig. 7.2 are visited if (a) $v =$ vertex 1, (b) $v =$ vertex 4. In both cases, when you have a choice of which vertex to visit next, choose the one with the smallest label.

2 Consider a maze such as that shown in Fig. 7.3 (on page 94). The notion of backtracking should suggest an algorithm to find a path through the maze from Enter to Exit or, if none exists, to indicate this fact. Sketch such an algorithm.

3 Another application of backtracking is to the *eight queens* problem which is to place eight queens on a chessboard so that no two attack each other (i.e. no two are in the same row or column or on the same diagonal). Consider trying to do this by placing the first queen somewhere in the first column, then placing the second queen in the second column so that it does not attack the first queen etc. Show how backtracking can be used for an algorithm to solve this problem. (Backtracking is a generally very important algorithmic idea whose power we have only been able to suggest.)

4 Corresponding to depth first search there is *breadth first search* in which we first visit those vertices closest to the starting vertex (i.e. adjacent to this vertex), then those next closest etc. Sketch a non-recursive algorithm for breadth first search. What is the order in which the vertices are visited in breadth first search for the graph of Fig. 7.2 starting at vertex 1?

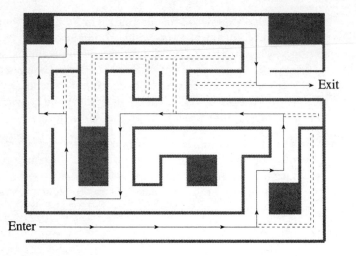

Figure 7.3: A maze: the thicker lines represent walls, the line with arrows is the path through the maze and the dashed lines show paths which lead to dead ends.

3 Graph colouring

Suppose you are a school official with the task of scheduling examinations so that no student has two examinations at the same time. Consider a graph in which the vertices represent examinations and an edge between two vertices represents a student who must take both examinations. If we then associate a *colour* with each vertex, with different colours representing different examination times, the desired schedule will be such that no two adjacent vertices have the same colour. If the number of possible examination times is limited, you would wish to use a minimum number of colours.

The problem described above is an exemplar of a class of problems which depend on colouring a graph with the minimum possible number of colours. This minimum is called the *chromatic number* of the graph. Finding a minimum colouring of a graph (i.e. a colouring in which the number of colours equals the chromatic number)

is a very difficult problem. In this section we present Algorithm
7.3 which is a plausible approach to colouring a graph with a near
minimum number of colours. Instead of using actual colours, we
shall represent colours by the integers 1, 2, ...

Input G [A graph]

Algorithm COLOURGRAPH

> Choose an arbitrary vertex v in G and colour it 1
> $V' \leftarrow V - \{v\}$ [V is the set of vertices of G]
> **repeat while** $V' \neq \emptyset$ [$\emptyset$ is the empty set]
> $u \leftarrow$ an arbitrary vertex in V' [So u not yet coloured]
> $S \leftarrow A(u)$ [$A(u)$ is set of vertices adjacent to u]
>   Colour u the minimum colour not yet assigned
>   to a vertex in S
> $V' \leftarrow V' - \{u\}$ [New set of uncoloured vertices]
> **endrepeat**
> $k \leftarrow$ maximum colour assigned to a vertex

Output k and colour of each vertex in V

Algorithm 7.3: Colouring a graph

We have used standard set notation in this algorithm in which
$V - W$ is the set V with all elements of the set W removed from
it. So $V - \{v\}$ means the set consisting of V with v removed.

■ EXERCISE 7.3

1 Show the result of applying COLOURGRAPH to the graph of Fig.
7.2 if (a) $v =$ vertex 1, and (b) $v =$ vertex 3. Choose the vertices
in numerical order of their labels [in (b): 3, 4, ..., 9, 1, 2].
2 Display a graph for which the output k of COLOURGRAPH is
greater than the chromatic number of the graph.

3 Graph colouring was at the heart of the proof of the famous Four Colour Theorem which (roughly) states that any map consisting of territories which abut one another, like the counties of England or the states of the United States (excepting Alaska and Hawaii), can be coloured with no more than four colours in such a way that no two territories with a common boundary have the same colour. (If three or more territories meet at a point, this does not count as a common boundary. This actually happens in the United States where four western states meet at a point.) But a map is not a graph so how can the material of this section apply to the Four Colour Theorem? (**Hint:** Show that any map can be converted to a graph by letting each vertex of the graph represent a territory on the map. Then what would the edges represent?)

4 Consider a graph which consists of a single *cycle*, that is a sequence of edges which form a circle so that, if there are n edges, there are also n vertices. (In general, a cycle is a path that begins and ends at the same vertex without traversing any edge more than once.) The chromatic number of such a graph depends upon a particular property of n. What is it and what is the chromatic number as a function of this property? (**Hint:** Consider such graphs for small n and work out their chromatic numbers.) What values of k may be obtained when COLOUR-GRAPH is applied to this class of graphs (as a function of n)?

4 Minimum spanning trees

Suppose you wanted to build a road network in an undeveloped country. The network must join together the n major cities of the country and must have the property that there is a path from any one city to any other, although that path may pass through intermediate cities. The cost of the network will be determined by the sum of the distances of all the city-to-city links in the network. Of course, you know the distances between each pair of cities. The question is: what cities should you link up directly (i.e. with a road between them which does not pass through any other city) to minimize the cost of the network?

It should be clear that this problem can be expressed in terms of a graph. An example is shown in Fig. 7.4. This *complete graph* (because it has all possible edges between pairs of vertices) has five vertices and ten edges. (In general, if a complete graph has *n* vertices, how many edges does it have (Q2))? So our question can be formulated as: which edges should be part of the network so that the graph is connected and so that the sum of the edge *weights* (which, in this example, are just the distances between cities) is minimized?

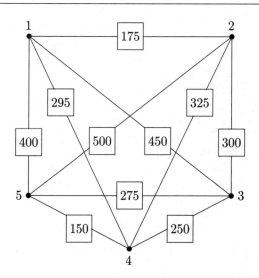

Figure 7.4: A sample graph for MINSPANTREE

Do you see that the graph consisting just of the edges in the network must not have any cycles? For, if there were a cycle, any one edge on the cycle could be deleted without disconnecting the graph. (Think about this!) A *tree* is a connected graph without any cycles. So we wish to find a tree, with all its edges from the given graph, which *spans* the graph, that is, it contains all the vertices of the original graph. In addition, among all possible *spanning trees*, we want the one for which the edge weights have the minimum sum. Such a tree is called a *minimum spanning tree* (MST).

The key to finding a minimum spanning tree is a theorem –
which we won't prove – that, as you build such a tree, vertex by
vertex, it is always the case that the shortest (i.e. the smallest
weight) edge which joins a vertex already on the tree to a vertex not
yet on the tree must be on the minimum spanning tree. Algorithm
7.4 implements this idea.

Input G [Graph with vertex set V]
       W [The set of weights for each edge]

Algorithm MINSPANTREE

    Find the edge $\{l, m\}$ with minimum weight among
        all edges; break ties arbitrarily
    $T \leftarrow \{l, m, \{l, m\}\}$ [Vertices l, m, edge $\{l, m\}$ initialize T]
    $U \leftarrow V - \{l\} - \{m\}$ [U is set of unused vertices]
    repeat until $U = \emptyset$
        Find the minimum weight edge $\{q, k\}$ among all
            edges from a vertex q in T to a vertex k not in T;
            break ties arbitrarily
        $T \leftarrow T \cup \{k, \{q, k\}\}$ [Add vertex k, edge $\{q, k\}$ to T]
        $U \leftarrow U - \{k\}$ [Remove k from unused set]
    endrepeat

Output T [List of vertices and edges on MST]

Algorithm 7.4: Minimum spanning tree

Note the use of $\{l, m\}$ to represent an edge. Since G is a graph,
its edges do not have a direction. Therefore, we use set notation
($\{\ldots\}$) to represent an edge since this implies no preferred order
for l and m (i.e. $\{l, m\}$ is the same edge as $\{m, l\}$).

■ **EXERCISE 7.4**

1 This algorithm is one of a class called *greedy* algorithms. Can you think of a reason for using this word?

Answer Because a greedy algorithm takes the path of least resistance, always doing the easiest thing, in this case always adding the shortest length edge between T and U. It is rather unusual for a greedy algorithm to be the best algorithm for solving a problem, but in this case it is.

2 Apply MINSPANTREE to the graph of Fig. 7.4.

3 Suppose instead of adding the shortest edge between T and U you just add the shortest edge not yet part of T, the only proviso being that the edge added does not form a cycle with edges already on the tree. (In a sense this algorithm is even greedier than MINSPANTREE!) Will this modified algorithm find the MST or not? Apply this algorithm to the graph of Fig. 7.4.

The four algorithms in this chapter are, although fairly characteristic of graph algorithms generally, just a tiny sampling of this very broad and important class of algorithms.

■ **ANSWERS TO QUESTIONS**

Q1 The idea of depth first search is that, each time you reach a vertex not previously visited, in effect, you treat that vertex as the starting vertex of a *subgraph* consisting of all vertices of the graph connected to the starting vertex but not yet visited. Then you apply depth first search to that subgraph. So, you keep applying the idea of depth first search to successively smaller subgraphs (i.e. subgraphs with fewer vertices) until you arrive at a subgraph where the starting vertex is the only vertex on the subgraph. Then you visit this vertex and backtrack to the starting vertex of the previous subgraph to see if there are any more subgraphs to be visited, starting there. The idea of going to successively smaller cases (i.e. subgraphs) until you arrive at a case – a subgraph with a single vertex – to which you know the solution is a characteristic of all recursive algorithms.

Q2 The answer is the number of *combinations* of n things taken two at a time which is $n(n + 1)/2$.

■ ANSWERS TO EXERCISES

Exercise 7.1

1 The path matrix which results is

$$\begin{bmatrix} 2 & 5 & 1 & 3 & 1 & 2 \\ 5 & 2 & 6 & 5 & 6 & 0 \\ 1 & 6 & 0 & 1 & 0 & 4 \\ 3 & 5 & 1 & 2 & 1 & 2 \\ 1 & 6 & 0 & 1 & 0 & 4 \\ 2 & 0 & 4 & 2 & 4 & 0 \end{bmatrix}$$

2 Between 1 and 4: 1214, 1414, 1424
Between 3 and 6: 3636, 3232, 3256, 3656

Exercise 7.2

1 a) This table, in which ∅ represents the empty set, is the answer.

Vertex visited (v) or returned to (r)	Adjacent set not visited
v1	{2, 4, 5}
v2	{3,5}
v3	∅
r2	{5}
v5	{4,8}
v4	{6,7}
v6	{7,9}
v7	∅
r6	{9}
v9	∅
r6	∅
r4	∅
r5	{8}
v8	∅
r5	∅
r2	∅
r1	∅

b) An abbreviated version of the table for (1a) is: visit vertices 4, 1, 2, 3; then backtrack to 2; visit 5,7,6,9; backtrack to 6,7,5; visit 8.

2 Input A maze

Algorithm MAZEPATH

> **procedure** TRAVERSE(P)   [P is a path in maze]
> > Go as far as possible always choosing the right-most
> > > untraversed fork
> > **if** Exit reached **then print** 'success'; **stop**
> > > > **else** Back up to last fork with
> > > > > untraversed path P*
> > > > > > TRAVERSE(P*)
> **endif**
> **endpro**

> TRAVERSE(E)   [E is right-most path at Enter]
> **print** 'failure'   [No path if ever return to initial call]

Output 'success' or 'failure'
Actually, you would also want to record the successful path if there is one.

3 Here is a sketch of the eight queens algorithm.

Place Q(ueen)1 on S(quare)1, F(ile) 1.
Place Q2 on the first available S in F2 (actually S3).
Continue placing Qs in successive files until there is no
> square available (actually in F6).
Backtrack to the first F where there is another space
> available for a Q (removing Qs in each
> F returned to).
Then move forward as above.
Continue moving forward and backtracking until a Q
> is placed in F8.

4 Here is an algorithm for breadth first search. The notion of a *queue*, which appears in this algorithm, is that of a data structure where items are inserted at one end (the 'back') and removed from the other end (the 'front').

Input G

Algorithm BFS

    Mark all vertices 'not visited'
    Choose a starting vertex v arbitrarily
    Visit v and mark v 'visited'
    Put v on Q [Q is a queue]
    repeat while $Q \neq \emptyset$ [Empty queue has no items on it]
        $u \leftarrow \text{head}(Q)$ [head(Q) is item at front]
        for w in $A(u)$
                  [$A(u)$ is set of vertices adjacent to u]
           if w not visited **then**
                Visit w; mark w 'visited'
                Put w on Q [That is, at the back of Q]
          endif
        endfor
        Delete u from Q [All neighbours visited]
    endrepeat

Output Results of processing information at each vertex

The breadth first search order for the graph of Fig. 7.2 starting at vertex 1 is 1, 2, 4, 5, 3, 6, 7, 8, 9.

Exercise 7.3

1 When $v =$ vertex 1:

Vertex:	1	2	3	4	5	6	7	8	9
Colour:	1	2	1	2	3	1	4	1	2

When $v =$ vertex 3:

Vertex:	3	4	5	6	7	8	9	1	2
Colour:	1	1	2	2	3	1	1	3	4

2 One answer is the graph of Fig. 7.2! Here is a colouring of the graph of Fig. 7.2 which only requires three colours.

Vertex:	1	2	3	4	5	6	7	8	9
Colour:	1	2	1	2	3	3	1	1	1

3 There would be edges between any two vertices (i.e. territories) which have a common boundary.

4 If n is even, the chromatic number of the graph is 2 since vertices may be coloured alternately around the cycle. But if n is odd, the chromatic number is 3 because with alternate colouring, the first vertex and second from the end have different colours. COLOURGRAPH always gives $k = 3$ if n is odd but it can give 2 or 3 if n is even.

Exercise 7.4

2 The edges are added in the order (4,5), (3,4), (4,1), (1,2).

3 Applied to the graph of Fig. 7.4 the edges are added in the order (4,5), (1,2), (3,4), (1,4) which gives the same minimum spanning tree as MINSPANTREE. And, yes, this algorithm also always gives the minimum spanning tree.

8

Algorithms from calculus

This chapter is mainly for readers who have some knowledge of calculus. However, even for those who do not, the first two algorithms should be instructive as long as you understand that their purpose is to find the area under a curve, that is the shaded area in Figure 8.1. For the third algorithm in this chapter, you will need some knowledge of calculus to make complete sense of it but even without this knowledge, the algorithm to be presented should be understandable and instructive.

1 The trapezoidal rule and Simpson's rule

The process of integration in calculus is used to find the area under a curve between $x = a$ and $x = b$ defined by a function $f(x)$ using *analytic* means, that is, by finding another function $g(x)$ such that $g(b) - g(a)$ gives the desired area. Mathematicians have long recognized that, far more often than not, it is not possible to find such a function $g(x)$ so, long before the advent of computers, they searched for *numerical* methods by which the area could be *approximated* as closely as desired. Before the advent of computers, the limited computational facilities available necessitated simple numerical methods which did not involve large calculations. This section is about two such methods which still are applicable in the computer age because simple methods that were used before computers were available are often also powerful methods when they are used with the full computational power of a computer.

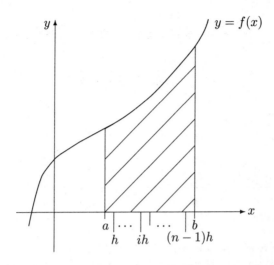

Figure 8.1: The area under a curve; the labels h, ih and $(n-1)h$ represent distances from a.

In Fig. 8.1 we have divided the interval $[a, b]$ into n equal sub-intervals, each of length $h = (b-a)/n$. In Fig. 8.2 (on page 106) we focus on two such intervals in order to illustrate both the methods we are going to present, the *trapezoidal rule* (called the *trapezium rule* in the United Kingdom) and *Simpson's rule*. In the left portion of Fig. 8.2, in order to approximate the area under the curve (shown shaded), we consider the trapezoid whose top line extends from $f(a+ih)$ to $f(a+(i+1)h)$. If you recall the formula for the area of a trapezoid, then you will know that the area of the trapezoid formed by this top line, the lines $x = a + ih$ and $x = a + (i+1)h$ and the x-axis is $\frac{1}{2}h[f(a+ih) + f(a+(i+1)h)]$. If h is quite small (so that the number of intervals is large), then the top line will closely approximate the curve and so the area of the trapezoid will closely approximate the area under the curve.

If we now use such a trapezoid to approximate the area under the curve in each of the n intervals and then add all the areas

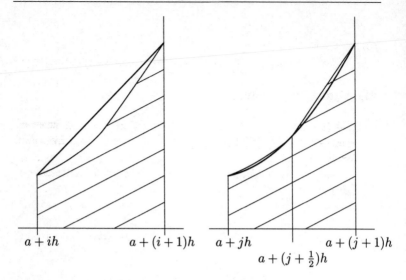

Figure 8.2: The trapezoidal rule and Simpson's rule; the thin lines are $f(x)$ and the thicker ones are the approximations.

---

together, we obtain the trapezoidal rule approximation to the area under the curve (called the *integral* of $f(x)$ and denoted by the symbol $\int$) from $x = a$ to $x = b$.

$$\int_a^b f(x)dx \approx \frac{h}{2}f(a) + h\sum_{i=1}^{n-1} f(a + ih) + \frac{h}{2}f(b).$$

Note that all the values of $f(a + ih)$ appear in the areas of two trapezoids except for the values at a and b.

By choosing n sufficiently large (and how large depends upon $f(x)$), the accuracy of this approximation can be made as good as desired. Algorithm 8.1 implements the trapezoidal rule. It assumes the existence of a separate procedure, which is not shown, which computes the value of $f(x)$ for any value of x supplied to it.

For many integrals the trapezoidal rule is very effective because n can be made very large without requiring a great amount of computation. Still, there are cases where the accuracy required is so great that the trapezoidal rule would be quite inefficient. Simpson's

Input n, a, b

    $f(x)$ [That is, the procedure to compute $f(x)$]

Algorithm TRAPEZOID

    $h \leftarrow (b-a)/n$ [Width of each interval]

    $sum \leftarrow (f(a) + f(b))/2$ [Initialize *sum*]

    for $i = 1$ **to** $n - 1$

        $sum \leftarrow sum + f(a + ih)$ [Form sum as above]

    endfor

    $sum \leftarrow h * sum$

Output *sum*   [The approximate integral]

Algorithm 8.1: The trapezoidal rule

Rule applies the essential idea of the trapezoidal rule to obtain a more accurate method.

In the right half of Fig. 8.2 we show an approximation to the curve in an interval, not by a straight line through the two endpoints but rather by a parabola which not only passes through both endpoints (i.e. the points $(a+jh, f(a+jh))$ and $(a+(j+1)h, f(a+(j+1)h)))$ but also through the point at the midpoint of the interval $(a+(j+1/2)h, f(a+(j+1/2)h)))$. Such a parabola can always be found and then the area under it can be found. We won't do this because it involves a lot of tedious algebra and calculus. The result, again found by adding up the areas for each interval (now bounded by a parabola at the top), is

$$\int_a^b f(x)dx \approx \frac{h}{6}f(a) + \frac{h}{3}\sum_{i=1}^{n-1} f(a+ih) + \frac{2h}{3}\sum_{i=0}^{n-1} f(a+(i+\frac{1}{2})h) + \frac{h}{6}f(b).$$

This formula, called Simpson's rule, can be turned into an algorithm similar to TRAPEZOID but we shall leave this to you in the Exercise which follows. Suffice it to say here that, because a parabola generally gives a better fit to the actual curve than a straight line, Simpson's rule is usually more accurate than the trapezoidal rule for a given value of n. (Sometimes the interval over which the curve is approximated by a parabola is taken to be $2h$ rather than h; we have used the latter here to make clearer the comparison of Simpson's rule with the trapezoidal rule.)

■ EXERCISE 8.1

1 Write the algorithm for Simpson's rule analogous to TRAPEZOID.
2 Hand trace both TRAPEZOID and the algorithm you wrote for (1) for $f(x) = x^3, a = 0, b = 1$ first with $n = 2$ and then with $n = 4$ and 6. For each n, which gives the more accurate answer? (The true answer is $\frac{1}{4}$.) Did you get successively more accurate answers with $n = 4$ and 6 for each method?
3 For what functions $f(x)$ would you expect the trapezoidal rule and Simpson's rule to give exact results (i.e. the same results as analytic integration), assuming that you could carry out all the arithmetic with perfect precision?
4 If you wanted a method which would be still more accurate than either the trapezoidal rule or Simpson's rule for a given value of n, what might you try?

2 Romberg's method

An important algorithmic technique is to use multiple approximations you have calculated for a single problem to find a better approximation than any of them. Romberg's method epitomizes this idea.

Suppose you have used the trapezoidal rule for a function $f(x)$ on an interval $[a, b]$ for the following sequence of values of n:

$$2^0(= 1), 2^1, 2^2, 2^3, \ldots, 2^{m-1}, 2^m.$$

So you have computed the trapezoidal rule $m + 1$ times, each time using twice as many intervals as the previous time. Can you use the resulting $m + 1$ approximations to get a better approximation than any of them? Almost always, the answer is, yes. Before we show you how to do it – unfortunately, we haven't got the space to show you why it works – we need some notation. Let T_{0k} represent the trapezoidal rule result with 2^k intervals. Then define

$$T_{rk} = \frac{1}{4^r - 1}(4^r T_{r-1,k+1} - T_{r-1,k}), \quad \begin{aligned} r &= 1, 2, \ldots, m \\ k &= 0, 1, \ldots, m - r \end{aligned}$$

If you've never seen a *recurrence relation* like this before, study it carefully. With $r = 1$ you compute $T_{10}, T_{11}, \ldots, T_{1,m-1}$ using the trapezoidal rule values $T_{01}, T_{02}, \ldots, T_{0m}$. Then with $r = 2$, the last term computed, using the just-computed values of T_{1i}, is $T_{2,m-2}$. Finally, with $r = m$, you compute only T_{m0} and this is our better approximation. Algorithm 8.2 captures this idea and uses TRAPEZOID as a function subalgorithm with a parameter, the number of intervals to be used.

Input $n, a, b, f(x), m$ [With m the Romberg parameter]

Algorithm ROMBERG

    for $k = 0$ **to** m
        $T_{0k} \leftarrow$ TRAPEZOID(2^k)   [Do $m + 1$ trapezoidal rules]
    endfor
    for $r = 1$ **to** m
        for $k = 0$ **to** $m - r$
            $T_{rk} \leftarrow [1/(4^r - 1)](4^r T_{r-1,k+1} - T_{r-1,k})$
                              [From Romberg equation]
        endfor
    endfor

Output T_{m0} [The Romberg approximation]

Algorithm 8.2: Romberg's method

You'll only really understand this algorithm if you actually use it. So we'll get straight to the exercise.

■ **EXERCISE 8.2**

1 Hand trace ROMBERG for $f(x) = x^3, a = 0, b = 1$ and $m = 3$. Remember that you already have the results for two and four intervals from (1) of Exercise 8.1. What do you conclude about the accuracy of ROMBERG for this function?

2 Now hand trace ROMBERG for $f(x) = \sin x, a = 0, b = \pi$ and $m = 2$.

*3 If you choose m larger than necessary for the level of accuracy you wish to achieve, then you will do a lot of unnecessary computation in ROMBERG. However, it is not necessary first to compute all the trapezoidal rules and then compute the values of T_{rk}. As soon as you have computed T_{01} you can compute T_{10} and then, after computing T_{02}, you can compute T_{11} and T_{20}. So modify ROMBERG so that each time a new T_{0k} is computed, you then compute T_{k0}.

4 To make the result of (3) useful you need some criterion for stopping the computation when a desired level of accuracy had been achieved. Modify the result of (3) so that the computation terminates when the magnitude of the difference of two successive values of T_{k0} is less than an input parameter ϵ.

*5 Did you notice that each trapezoidal rule computation requires re-evaluation of $f(x)$ at some points at which it has already been evaluated in previous trapezoidal rule computations? How might you take advantage of this fact to reduce the total amount of computation in ROMBERG?

3 Symbolic differentiation

Calculators and computers can now perform symbolic as well as numeric calculations. That is, they can accept input in the form of symbols rather than numbers and can output symbolic results. We've already given, essentially, an example of this in POLYMULT where the (numerical) input was the coefficients of two polynomials and the (numeric) output was the coefficients of the product polynomial. But the output *could* have been the entire product polynomial, not just its coefficients. We'll come back to this point in Exercise 8.3 below.

Among the things calculators and computers can do symbolically is differentiate. That is, given as input a function $f(x)$ which is any combination (using arithmetic and radicals) of elementary functions (i.e. polynomial, trigonometric, exponential and logarithmic), the output will be the derivative of the input function. An algorithm to do this task in the generality we have just stated would be long and complex. So in this section we shall consider only a small piece of this problem, namely the differentiation of polynomials. Even if you don't know anything about differentiation, you should be able to understand this algorithm since all you need to know is that given a polynomial

$$P(x) = a_n x^n + a_{n-1} x^{n-1} + \cdots + a_1 x + a_0 = \sum_{i=0}^{n} a_i x^i$$

its derivative is given by

$$P'(x) = n a_n x^{n-1} + (n-1) a_{n-1} x^{n-2} + \cdots + 2 a_2 x + a_1 = \sum_{i=1}^{n} i a_i x^{i-1}.$$

From this equation, Algorithm 8.3 (on page 112) for differentiating a polynomial follows easily.

Pay especial attention to the intermixture of literals (in inverted commas) and names of variables in the **print** statements in the loop so that you're sure you understand just what is supposed to be printed out. We have not, by the way, made any provision in our AL for terminating one line of output and beginning a new one. We could have done so but chose not to for the sake of simplicity. It is, of course, the intention in POLYDIFF that the entire derivative polynomial be output on one line.

■ EXERCISE 8.3

1 For each $P(x)$ that follows, state what should be output by POLYDIFF. Make sure every symbol is as it is supposed to be.

- $P(x) = 7x^4 - 5x^3 + 3x^2 + 2x - 7$
- $P(x) = -3x^3 + 4x + 1$

Input $n; a_i, i = 0, 1, \ldots, n$ [Degree and coefficients of polynomial]

Algorithm POLYDIFF

    for $i = 0$ **to** $n - 1$
        $b_i \leftarrow (i + 1)a_{i+1}$ [b_i is coefficient of x^i in $P'(x)$]
    endfor
    print '$P'(x) = $'
    for $i = n - 1$ **downto** 0
      if $b_i \geq 0$ **then**
        print ' + 'b_i'x'^{i}
             else
        $b_i \leftarrow -b_i$ [Change b_i to positive number]
        print ' $-$ 'b_i'x'^{i}
      endif
    endfor

Output $P'(x) = b_{n-1}x^{n-1} + b_{n-2}x^{n-2} + \cdots + b_1 x + b_0$
                                [With coefficients as numbers]

Algorithm 8.3: Symbolic differentiation

---

2 You may have noticed that POLYDIFF has some unfortunate aspects in terms of how the output appears. In any case, (1) should have emphasized these. What aspects of how POLYDIFF outputs its results are a bit unfortunate? Show how to modify POLYDIFF to avoid these infelicities.

3 Show how to modify POLYMULT from Chapter 4 so that it outputs not just the coefficients of the product polynomial but rather the polynomial itself as in POLYDIFF.

To design an algorithm to do differentiation more generally, when $f(x)$ can have powers of x and exponentials and log functions and trigonometric functions all intermixed, is clearly far more difficult than it is when $f(x)$ can only be a polynomial. But it is quite possible. Such an algorithm lies at the heart of the calculus portion of the symbolic systems now available on computers and calculators.

■ ANSWERS TO EXERCISES

Exercise 8.1

1 Input $n, a, b, f(x)$

Algorithm SIMPSON

$h \leftarrow (b - a)/n$
$sum \leftarrow f(a) + f(b)$
for $i = 1$ **to** $n - 1$
    $sum \leftarrow sum + 2f(a + ih)$
endfor
for $i = 0$ **to** $n - 1$
    $sum \leftarrow sum + 4f(a + (i + 1/2)h)$
endfor
$sum \leftarrow h * sum/6$

Output *sum*

2 For TRAPEZOID: 0.3125 for $n = 2$, 0.265625 for $n = 4$, 0.256944 for $n = 6$. For SIMPSON: 0.25 for $n = 2$, 4 and 6. So TRAPEZOID gives successively more accurate answers but SIMPSON is exact for each value of n.

3 TRAPEZOID is exact for linear functions (i.e. straight line graphs) and SIMPSON is exact for quadratic functions (i.e. parabolas) because each was designed to fit those functions exactly. It turns out that SIMPSON is also exact for cubics.

4 The obvious option would be to fit a higher degree polynomial, such as a cubic or quartic, to $f(x)$ over each interval of width h.

Exercise 8.2

1 The array of values for T_{rk}, where r goes from 0 to 3 down the columns and k goes from 0 to 3 across the rows, is:

0.5	0.3125	0.265625	0.25390625
0.25	0.25	0.25	
0.25	0.25		
0.25			

The reason all values below those in the top row give the exact answer is that Romberg's method is such that T_{rk} is exact for polynomials of degree $r+1$ and, in fact, T_{1k} is exact for cubics.

2 The array, similar to that for (1), is:

0.0   1.570796   1.896119
2.094395   2.004560
1.998571

3 Replace the algorithm part of ROMBERG with

$T_{00} \leftarrow$ TRAPEZOID(1)   [Or just $(f(a)+f(b))/2$]
for $k=1$ **to** m
    $T_{0k} \leftarrow$ TRAPEZOID(2^k)
    for $r=1$ **to** k
        $T_{r,k-r} \leftarrow [1/(4^r-1)](4^r T_{r-1,k-r+1} - T_{r-1,k-r})$
    endfor
endfor

4 Add a quantity ϵ to the input and enclose everything after the first statement in the answer to (3) in a loop:

repeat
    $\vdots$
endrepeat when $|T_{0k} - T_{0,k-1}| < \epsilon$

where $|\ldots|$ represents the *absolute value* function which equals its argument when that argument is positive and is the negative of the argument when the argument is negative.

5 You could just store the values of $f(x)$ as you compute them and then use them when they are needed. But a cleverer way is to note that $T_{0,k+1}$ uses the same points as T_{0k} at which to evaluate $f(x)$ plus those points half way in between the points used for T_{0k}. Thus,

$$T_{0,k+1} = \frac{1}{2}T_{0k} + h \sum_{i=0}^{2^k-1} f(a + (2i+1)h)$$

with $h = (b-a)/2^{k+1}$.

Exercise 8.3

1 For the first polynomial: $P'(x) = +28x^3 - 15x^2 + 6x^1 + 2x^0$.
For the second: $P'(x) = -9x^2 + 4x^0$.

2 The infelicities are that (a) you get a leading $+$ sign when the first coefficient is positive, (b) exponents of 1 and 0 are printed, (c) coefficients equal to 1 are printed, and (d) 0 coefficients are not suppressed. To avoid these replace the second **for**-loop by

```
flag ← 0
for i = n − 1 downto 0
    if bᵢ ≠ 0 then                [Suppress zero coefficients]
        if bᵢ < 0 then
            bᵢ ← −bᵢ; print '−'       [Negative coefficients]
        else
            if flag = 1 then print '+'   [Not leading coeff.]
        endif
        if flag = 0 then flag ← 1         [Reset flag]
        if bᵢ ≠ 1 or i = 0 then print bᵢ
                                   [Don't print coefficient = ±1]
        if i ≥ 2 then print 'x'ⁱ
            i = 1 then print 'x'          [No exponent 1]
        endif
    endif
endfor
```

3 Just add to the end of POLYMULT the algorithm you developed in (2) with $n − 1$ replaced by $m + n$.

9
Recursive algorithms

We've presented several recursive algorithms so far in this book but we probably haven't convinced you that such algorithms can be efficient alternatives to iterative algorithms (although DEPTH-FIRSTSEARCH is a good and efficient algorithm). In this chapter we are going to present two algorithms which are both recursive and very efficient compared to their iterative counterparts.

1 The Towers of Hanoi

This is the classic example of a recursive algorithm, familiar to almost all who have ever taken a course in computer science. It is also familiar, although not with this name, to millions of others who have played with a toy – or whose children have played with a toy – based on this problem.

The problem is illustrated in Fig. 9.1. On one of three poles is a stack (i.e. a 'tower') of n rings, each smaller than the one below it. The object is to move the rings *from* the pole they are originally on, *to* a designated one of the other two, while obeying the following rules. (i) Only one ring may be moved at a time. (ii) A larger ring may never be placed on top of a smaller ring. It may help you to get a feel for this problem if you try to solve it for small values of n, say 2, 3 and 4, using coins of different sizes for the rings and imaginary poles.

Perhaps you already see that this problem is a prime candidate for the *recursive paradigm* which, in effect, we introduced in Chapter 2: Jump into the middle of the problem and work your way out. This translates in this case to mean: Suppose you knew a solution

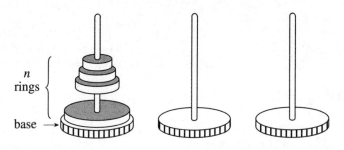

Figure 9.1: The Towers of Hanoi problem with the rings initially on Pole 1

when there were $n - 1$ rings. How would you find a solution for n rings? Well, suppose you wanted to move n rings from pole 1 to pole 3. Then use the known solution for $n - 1$ rings ('known' so far only in the sense that we have imagined we know it) to move $n - 1$ rings from pole 1 to pole 2. Then move the nth (i.e. bottom) ring to pole 3. Then use the known solution for $n - 1$ rings to move the $n - 1$ rings on pole 2 to pole 3. Do you see that the nth (and largest) ring never gets in the way of moving the $n - 1$ rings and that, therefore, this method will work? Try it first for some small values of n and then study Algorithm 9.1. In the algorithm $r \rightarrow s$ means move the top ring on pole r to pole s.

You should be familiar by now with the standard structure of a recursive algorithm in which a recursive subalgorithm is called from the main algorithm with the initial data of a problem. Another feature of any recursive algorithm which you see here is the 'escape' portion, that is the solution of the problem for the known simplest case which here is $n = 1$. In case you're puzzled by the $6 - r - s$ which appears twice, this is really just the use of a lucky accident, namely that if r and s are two of the three poles 1, 2 and 3, then $6 - r - s$ is the other pole.

Input *num*   [Number of rings]
   Pinit   [Initial pole; $1 \leq Pinit \leq 3$]
   Pfin   [Final pole; $1 \leq Pfin \leq 3, Pfin \neq Pinit$]

Algorithm HANOI

   procedure $H(n, r, s)$ [Subalgorithm to move n rings
      if $n = 1$ **then** $r \rightarrow s$ from pole r to pole s]
         else $H(n - 1, r, 6 - r - s)$
                        [Move $n - 1$ rings to unused pole]
                  $r \rightarrow s$ [Move bottom ring]
                  $H(n - 1, 6 - r - s, s)$
                        [Move $n - 1$ rings to final pole]
   endif
   return
   endpro

   $H(num, Pinit, Pfin)$ [Call of H from main algorithm]

Output List of commands $r \rightarrow s$

Algorithm 9.1: The Towers of Hanoi

■ **EXERCISE 9.1**

1 Hand trace HANOI with $num = 3, Pinit = 1, Pfin = 3$ to generate the ring moves to solve the problem.

Answer

In Fig. 9.2 we list both the calls of the procedure H as well as the actual moves themselves so that you can follow the execution. The indenting of the calls shows the levels (or depth) of the recursion.

   If you have followed our answer, you will understand how to figure out how recursive algorithms work in general.

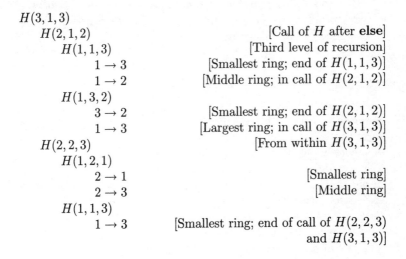

```
H(3, 1, 3)
   H(2, 1, 2)                            [Call of H after else]
      H(1, 1, 3)                         [Third level of recursion]
         1 → 3                 [Smallest ring; end of H(1, 1, 3)]
         1 → 2               [Middle ring; in call of H(2, 1, 2)]
      H(1, 3, 2)
         3 → 2                 [Smallest ring; end of H(2, 1, 2)]
         1 → 3             [Largest ring; in call of H(3, 1, 3)]
   H(2, 2, 3)                            [From within H(3, 1, 3)]
      H(1, 2, 1)
         2 → 1                                  [Smallest ring]
         2 → 3                                    [Middle ring]
      H(1, 1, 3)
         1 → 3        [Smallest ring; end of call of H(2, 2, 3)]
                                           and H(3, 1, 3)]
```

Figure 9.2: The calls of procedure H and the moves of the rings with $num = 3, Pinit = 1, Pfin = 3$

2 The correctness of recursive algorithms can often be proved by mathematical induction. Using the proposition $P(n)$: HANOI correctly solves the Towers of Hanoi problem for n rings, use the text of HANOI to prove the basis case $(n = 1)$ and then that $P(n - 1) \Rightarrow P(n)$.

3 For $n = 1, 2, \ldots, 7$, make a table of the number of moves of a ring from one pole to another, call it h_n, to solve the Towers of Hanoi problem. You needn't actually play out the game for each value of n; you should be able to use HANOI to work out the number of moves when there are n rings from the result for $n - 1$ rings. What pattern do you see in the values of h_n?

*4 Is there perhaps a better way (i.e. a way involving fewer ring moves) to solve the Towers of Hanoi problem? Suppose there were and let h_n^* be the number of moves for this best way. Then see if you can reason that h_n^* must be at least as great as h_n for any n, thus proving that HANOI is indeed the best possible algorithm to solve this problem. Finding a best possible algorithm for a problem, as we have here, is to solve the question of the *complexity* of an algorithm.

2 Quicksort

Suppose you were able to divide a list of distinct elements to be sorted into two equal – or almost equal – parts such that all the elements in one part were less than any element in the other part. Then you could sort each part separately and, indeed, you could apply this same idea recursively to each of the two parts: divide each part into two equal parts such that all the elements in one part are less than any element in the other part etc. until you get sublists with only one or two elements. In a sense, this is the strategy of binary search applied to sorting.

Sound good? Alas, it turns out to be as hard to divide a list into two equal parts as described above as it is to sort it by a method such as bubble sort or insertion sort. Still, there is the germ of a good idea here. If we are willing to give up dividing the list into two nearly equal parts but will settle instead just to divide it into parts where all the elements in one part are less than any element in the other, it turns out we are on to something, because it is easy to divide a list into two sublists such that all the elements in one sublist are less than any in the other. Although occasionally the two sublists will be very unequal in size (e.g. one element in one and all the rest in the other), often enough they are nearly enough the same size that the method works well. The method we have roughly described is called Quicksort (because it is quick) or, sometimes, *partition exchange sort* (because it exchanges elements between *partitions* which are just the sublists we have described above).

To be a little more specific now, let our list be L. As earlier, we shall focus on the keys associated with each list item rather than on the entire item. Our specific aim – slightly different from the description above – is to find a key k and two partitions (i.e. sublists) of L such that k is greater than (or equal to) each key in one partition and less than (or equal to) each in the other partition. PARTLIST is an algorithm which performs this task. It takes a sublist with its first element in position F and its last element in position L and places the element that was initially in position F in a new position p, such that now all keys in positions $F + 1, F + 2, \ldots, p - 1$ are less than (or equal to) the key in position p, and all elements in positions $p + 1, p + 2, \ldots, L$ are greater than (or equal to) the key in position p. As you will see Algorithm 9.2 does this in an efficient and elegant way. Our advice is: read the algorithm, which will almost certainly seem confusing at first, then look at Exercise 9.2 while reading the algorithm again. We have written this algorithm as a procedure subalgorithm because we shall use it just below in the full algorithm for Quicksort.

Input $n, K_i, i = 1, 2, \ldots, n$ [n is the number of keys]

procedure PARTLIST(F, L)

    $p \leftarrow F$ [Initialize position p to F]
    $i \leftarrow F + 1; j \leftarrow L$ [Initialize two pointers]
    repeat
        repeat until $K_p > K_j$ **or** $j = p$ [From the right,
            $j \leftarrow j - 1$ look for first $K_j < K_p$]
        endrepeat
        if $p < j$ **then** $K_p \leftrightarrow K_j; p \leftarrow j; j \leftarrow j - 1$ [Interchange]
            else exit   [**exit** if $p = j$]
        repeat until $K_p < K_i$ **or** $i = p$ [From the left,
            $i \leftarrow i + 1$ look for first $K_i > K_p$]
        endrepeat
        if $p > i$ **then** $K_p \leftrightarrow K_i; p \leftarrow i; i \leftarrow i + 1$ [Interchange]
            else exit   [**exit** if $p = i$]
    endrepeat
    return p [Position of pivot $\rightarrow$ calling algorithm]
endpro

Output A partitioned list

Algorithm 9.2: Partitioning a list

Note the p after **return**. Our AL allows a list of variables, separated by commas, after **return** to designate those values which are specifically returned to the calling algorithm. Also note the use of 'pointer' in one of the comments in PARTLIST. A *pointer* is just a variable which identifies (points to) a position in some data structure such as a list of items. We noted in Chapter 3 (p. 30) that a subscript is really a pointer into the elements of an array.

■ EXERCISE 9.2

1 Even if you don't understand yet how PARTLIST works, hand trace it for the following two data sets.
- 15   12   9   17   6   12   2   8   16
- 8   12   3   9   1   14   6   12   10   15   11

In each case use $F = 1$ and let L be the length of the list.

2 You should see now that what PARTLIST does first is take the first element in the list (sometimes called the *pivot* element) and, working from the right, move it to a position just to the left of all items at the end of the list greater than or equal to the pivot, by an exchange of the pivot with the first item less than the pivot. Then, working from the left, the pivot is moved to a position just to the right of items less than or equal to the pivot, this time exchanging the pivot with the first item greater than it. Then successively working from the right and left, the pivot finally ends up between two lists, one of items greater than or equal to it and the other of items less than or equal to it.

   At the end of each pass through the outer **repeat** ... **endrepeat** loop, four elements of the list may be identified: the position p of the pivot, a list T_1 of elements less than or equal to the pivot, a list T_2 of elements greater than or equal to the pivot, and a list T_3 of elements not yet compared with the pivot. For each of the two lists above, identify T_1, T_2 and T_3 after the first pass through the outer loop.

3 What happens if the first element of the list is less than all the other elements?

4 What happens if the first element is greater than all the other elements?

5 Relative to p, F and L, in what positions are the first and last elements of T_1 and T_2 at the end of the execution of PARTLIST? (This result is used in QUICKSORT below.)

Now that we have a procedure to partition the list, explaining the rest of Quicksort is easy. At the end of the execution of PARTLIST, the list has the form

$$T_1 \quad \text{pivot} \quad T_2$$

where T_1 and T_2 have the properties described above in (2) of Exercise 9.2. Now all we have to do is apply PARTLIST to T_1 and T_2 and continue doing so until the sublists obtained from PARTLIST are of length 0 or 1. This naturally recursive idea is encapsulated in Algorithm 9.3. Note that s and t are pointers to the first and last elements of the sublist being sorted at any stage. Initially $s = 1$ and $t = n$.

Input $n, K_i, i = 1, \ldots, n$

Algorithm QUICKSORT

> **procedure** QUICK(s, t)   [Recursive procedure]
> > **if** $t - s > 0$ **then**   [If $t - s \leq 0$, nothing to sort]
> > > PARTLIST(s, t)   [Apply PARTLIST to sublist]
> > > QUICK($s, p - 1$)   [Recursive call to sort T_1]
> > > QUICK($p + 1, t$)   [Recursive call to sort T_2]
> >
> > **endif**
> > **return**
> **endpro**

> QUICK(1,n)   [Main algorithm call of QUICK]

Output $K_1, K_2, \ldots, K_n$ in sorted order

Algorithm 9.3: Quicksort

QUICKSORT invokes two procedures, PARTLIST which we discussed above and QUICK which is the recursive procedure which accomplished the sorting. QUICKSORT is probably easier to understand than was PARTLIST but its recursive nature may well mean that it's not clear how all the recursive calls work. The first part of the next exercise should help to make this clear.

■ **EXERCISE 9.3**

1 Carry through QUICKSORT for both lists of (1) of Exercise 9.2. You will find it convenient to organize your work so that, beginning with the list itself, subsequent lines contain the calls of QUICK and PARTLIST with the result of PARTLIST appearing on the line after the call. These results should include only the partition of the sublist being operated on.

*2 But is all this worth it? That is, is Quicksort really better than Bubble Sort or Insertion Sort? The complete analysis is beyond us here but consider the following case: Suppose the original list has length $2^m - 1$ for some $m > 1$ and suppose each application of PARTLIST results in two sublists of equal length. Then answer the following.

  a) How many comparisons of list elements with the pivot is required in each application of PARTLIST to a list of length $2^j - 1$?

  b) Each application of PARTLIST to a list of length $2^j - 1$ results in two sublists of length $2^{j-1} - 1$. Why?

  c) So altogether how many sublists are there to be partitioned of length $2^{j-1} - 1, 2^{j-2} - 1, \ldots 7, 3$?

  d) Use the results of (a) and (c) to show that altogether the following number of comparisons is required

  $$(m-1)2^m - 2(1 + 2 + 4 + \cdots + 2^{m-2}) = m2^m - 2^{m+1} + 2.$$

  e) For large m the first term in the expression above is dominant. With $n = 2^m - 1$ show that this term can be written $(n+1)\log_2(n+1)$. This is much smaller than the n^2 which resulted from the analysis of Insertion Sort and Bubble Sort. It turns out that, although we have chosen to analyse a very special case and one which is especially favourable to Quicksort, the average number of comparisons for Quicksort is, in general, proportional to $n\log_2 n$ which means that Quicksort is far superior to Bubble Sort or Insertion Sort which, in turn, explains why it is so widely used on computers. [Recall that in the answer to 5.2(5) we compared the growth of n and $\log_2 n$.]

Quicksort is an exemplar of a *divide-and-conquer* algorithm in which we solve a problem by successively dividing it into smaller problems until we get to a case which we know how to solve trivially (in Quicksort how to sort a list of length 1). Another example of divide-and-conquer which we have seen is binary search. This very powerful algorithmic technique is applicable to very many problems.

■ ANSWERS TO EXERCISES

Exercise 9.1

2 The basis case is for $n = 1$ when H is called with $num = 1$ and explicitly moves the only ring from its starting pole r to its final pole s. For the inductive step, suppose that HANOI is correct for $n - 1$ rings. Then, when $num = n > 1$ and H is called, the three steps executed are:

$$H(n - 1, r, 6 - r - s)$$
$$r \rightarrow s$$
$$H(n - 1, 6 - r - s, s)$$

By the inductive hypothesis, the first line correctly moves the top $n - 1$ rings from the initial pole to the pole which is not the final one. Then the next step moves the largest ring from the initial pole to the final one. Finally, the third step correctly moves the $n - 1$ rings on the intermediate pole to the final one. Thus, the three steps together correctly move n rings. QED.

3 From HANOI you can see that $h_n = 2h_{n-1} + 1$ with $h_1 = 1$ so the table is:

n	1	2	3	4	5	6	7
h_n	1	3	7	15	31	63	127

The pattern implies that the formula for h_n is $h_n = 2^n - 1$.

4 Well, $h_1^* = 1$ because for one ring you can't do better than move it to the final pole. Now suppose $h_n^* < h_n$ with h_n as in (3). Any algorithm to solve the Towers of Hanoi problem must perforce at some point move the $n - 1$ rings to the intermediate pole, then move the largest ring to the final pole and then move the $n - 1$ rings to the final pole. So $h_n^* \geq 2h_{n-1}^* + 1$. But since h_n satisfies the equation given in (3), this means $h_n^* \geq h_n$. On the other hand, by assumption h_n^* is the smallest possible number of moves so $h_n^* \leq h_n$. The only possible conclusion is that $h_n^* = h_n$.

Exercise 9.2

1 For the first data set the result is 8, 12, 9, 2, 6, 12, $\boxed{15}$, 17, 16 with $p = 7$. The positions occupied by 15 before it reaches its final resting place are 1, 8 and 4. For the second data set the result is 6, 1, 3, $\boxed{8}$, 9, 14, 12, 12, 10, 15, 11 with $p = 4$ and with the other positions occupied by 8 being 1, 7, 2 and 5.
2 First data set: $T_1 = 8, 12, 9;$ $T_2 = 17, 16;$ $T_3 = 6, 12, 2.$ Second data set: $T_1 = 6;$ $T_2 = 12, 12, 10, 15, 11;$ $T_3 = 3, 9, 1, 14.$
3 Nothing happens; all elements stay where they were originally.
4 The first and last elements are exchanged and the rest stay where they were.
5 The first and last elements of T_1 are in positions F and $p - 1$, respectively, and those of T_2 are in positions $p + 1$ and L.

Exercise 9.3

1 The table at the top of the next page shows the results for the first data set. The indentations show the different levels of the recursion.

   For the second data set we give only the arguments of the successive calls of QUICK; from these you could produce a table like that for the first data set: (1,11), (1,3), (1,2), (1,1), (3,2), (4,3), (5,11), (5,4), (6,11), (6,9), (6,6), (8,9), (8,7), (9,9), (11,11).
2 (a) $2^j - 2$; (b) The two sublists have the same length, half of $2^j - 2$; (c) Respectively, $2, 4, 8, \ldots, 2^{j-2}$; (d) The first list requires $2^m - 2$ comparisons, the next two sublists of length $2^{m-1} - 1$ each require $2^m - 2$ comparisons. Continuing in this way for $m - 1$ terms gives the sum in the text. Since the sum in parentheses is $2^{m-1} - 1$, the right hand side of the equation in the text follows; (e) With $n = 2^m - 1$, $2^m = n + 1$ and $m = \log_2(n + 1)$.

```
15  12   9  17   6  12   2   8  16                    [Original list]
QUICK(1,9)
        PARTLIST(1,9)
 8  12   9   2   6  12 |15| 17  16                    [p = 7]
        QUICK(1,6)
                PARTLIST(1,6)
 6   2  |8|  9  12  12                                [p = 3]
                QUICK(1,2)
                        PARTLIST(1,2)
 2  |6|                                               [p = 2]
                        QUICK(1,1)
                QUICK(4,6)
                        PARTLIST(4,6)
            |9| 12  12                                [p = 4]
                        QUICK(5,6)
                                PARTLIST(5,6)
               |12| 12                                [p = 5]
                                QUICK(6,6)
        QUICK(8,9)
                PARTLIST(8,9)
                    16 |17|                           [p = 9]
                QUICK(8,8)

 2   6   8   9  12  12  16  17                    [Final sorted list]
```

10
Parallel algorithms

Whether you most commonly use a hand-held calculator or a personal computer, you are using a *serial* machine, one that executes one instruction after another and, in particular, executes only one instruction at a time. All our algorithms so far have been *serial algorithms* in which each statement was executed completely before proceeding on (or, in the case of **endrepeat** or **endfor**, back) to the next instruction.

For most calculations this serial mode is quite satisfactory; it gets the job done in a reasonable time. However, increasingly there are important calculations in science and technology for which this serial mode is just too slow. Matrices may be so large or loops may be repeated so many times that, even on the fastest computer, the calculation proceeds more slowly than can be accepted. This is especially true in *real time* calculations, such as, for example, space probes or controlling a chemical plant, where calculations must be completed at a particular time or lives or large investments may be at risk. Therefore, increasingly calculations are being performed on *parallel computers* in which multiple processors are connected so that each can perform a portion of a calculation simultaneously with partial results being communicated among them. The total number of processors can be counted in the thousands and, before long, parallel machines with hundreds of thousands or even millions of processors may be available.

In order to use such parallel processors effectively, algorithms must be couched in terms which enable them to be implemented efficiently and effectively on parallel machines. In this chapter we shall introduce you, albeit very briefly, to *parallel algorithms* so that you may get the flavour of what this subject of rapidly growing importance is about. To do this we shall introduce one additional structure to our AL. The **parallel ... endparallel** structure will be discussed in detail in the first example that follows.

1 Parallel summation

At the beginning of Chapter 2 (p. 14), we gave an algorithm fragment to compute the sum of n numbers. This algorithm required, as you would expect, $n - 1$ additions and, assuming the execution of each addition requires 1 unit of time, would take time proportional to $n - 1$ (or $O(n)$ to use a previous notation). (We say 'proportional' because, if the addition itself takes exactly one unit of time, the *overhead* of the computation would require some additional time for each addition, thus making the constant of proportionality somewhat greater than 1.)

Now suppose – to keep things as simple as possible – that we have n^2 numbers to be added which, added serially, would require $O(n^2)$ time. Suppose further that we consider these n^2 numbers to be made up of n sets of n numbers so that we may write the n^2 numbers as

$$a_{ij}, \quad i, j = 1, 2, \ldots, n.$$

Algorithm 10.1 uses a parallel approach to add these numbers.

The range of the parallelism variable (i in SUMPARALLEL) has precisely the same syntax as the range variable after **for**. For each value of the parallelism variable (with the step value implicitly 1 unless there is an explicit **step** quantity included), the statements between **parallel** and **endparallel** are to be executed *simultaneously*. Thus, in SUMPARALLEL the n partial sums b_i, each the sum of n values, are accumulated simultaneously. Our AL hides a number of issues which must be considered in any actual implementation on a computer. Which values of a_{ij} are stored in which processor? How are the various processors connected together (their *architecture*) and how do they communicate with one another? Since our focus here is on the parallelism itself rather than its implementation, we shall not discuss these matters further except to say that there are now several answers to our questions embodied in various parallel architectures and programming systems.

Before attempting the exercise which follows, study the algorithm SUMPARALLEL carefully to ensure that you understand how the sum is computed.

Input $n, a_{ij}, i, j = 1, 2, \ldots, n$

Algorithm SUMPARALLEL

> **parallel** $i = 1$ **to** n
> $\quad b_i \leftarrow a_{i1}$ [Initialize partial sum variables]
> $\quad$ **for** $j = 2$ **to** n
> $\quad\quad b_i \leftarrow b_i + a_{ij}$
> $\quad$ **endfor**
> **endparallel**
> $sum \leftarrow 0$ [Initialize sum]
> **for** $i = 1$ **to** n
> $\quad sum \leftarrow sum + b_i$ [Accumulate partial sums]
> **endfor**

Output sum

Algorithm 10.1: Parallel addition

■ **Exercise 10.1**

1 Hand trace SUMPARALLEL for the following data sets which are presented in the order

$$a_{11} a_{12} \cdots a_{1n} a_{21} \cdots a_{2n} \cdots a_{nn}.$$

- $4 \; -17 \; 32 \quad 6 \; 0 \; -12 \quad 14 \; -8 \; -5$
- $-2 \; 0 \; 14 \; 7 \quad 8 \; -3 \; -6 \; 2 \quad 7 \; 10 \; -5 \; -8 \quad -11 \; -15 \; 13 \; 20$

2 Assume that each addition takes one unit of time and ignore all other operations (such as the initializations) and the overhead we mentioned earlier. As a function of n, how many units of time are required to execute SUMPARALLEL? How does this compare with serial addition?

3 Now suppose the number of items to be added is not a perfect square. Can a parallel algorithm still be used to perform the addition of these items? If so, how? If not, why not?

4 Can we do even better than SUMPARALLEL? Try this. For convenience, let $n = 2^m$. Devise an algorithm for adding n numbers which adds 2^{m-1} pairs in parallel, then takes the 2^{m-1} results and adds them in parallel etc. until, at the last step, there are only two numbers to be added. Try to write this algorithm in AL. Even if you can't do this, how many time units would be required? Is it possible to speed things up even more than was achieved by the algorithm written to solve this problem if your computer hardware is not capable of adding together more than two numbers at a time?

5 Sometimes calculations which look like they have to be done serially can be done faster with a parallel approach. Consider the recurrence (see p. 125): $h_n = 2h_{n-1} + 1$ with $h_1 = 1$. By writing $h_n = 2(2h_{n-2}+1)+1$ show how the even and odd terms of $\{h_n\}$ can be computed in parallel.

2 Parallel matrix multiplication

Exercise 10.1 shows that, using parallelism, n^2 items can be added in $2n$ units of time, rather than the $n^2 - 1$ required for serial addition. Can the same approach be applied to achieve even more startling savings? The answer is, yes, and our second example in this chapter is an illustration of this.

We presented a serial algorithm, MATRIXMULT, for matrix multiplication in Chapter 6 (p. 74) and also showed there (Exercise 6.1) that to multiply two $n \times n$ matrices requires n^3 multiplications or, if a multiplication requires one unit if time, about n^3 units of time. So, in this context, consider the Algorithm 10.2 for parallel matrix multiplication.

As we hope you would expect, **parallel** ... **endparallel** structures can be nested just like loop structures. The nesting above means that the statements inside the two **parallel** ... **endparallel** structures are executed in parallel for all values of i *and* j. Thus, all n^2 values of c_{ij} are computed simultaneously.

Input $n, a_{ij}, b_{ij}, i, j = 1, 2, \ldots, n$

Algorithm MATRIXMULTPARALLEL

> **parallel** $i = 1$ **to** n
> > **parallel** $j = 1$ **to** n
> > > $c_{ij} \leftarrow a_{i1}b_{1j}$ [Initialize elements of $C = AB$]
> > > **for** $k = 2$ **to** n
> > > > $c_{ij} \leftarrow c_{ij} + a_{ik}b_{kj}$
> > >
> > > **endfor**
> >
> > **endparallel**
>
> **endparallel**

Output $C = [c_{ij}]$

Algorithm 10.2: Parallel matrix multiplication

■ **Exercise 10.2**

1 Show how you would use MATRIXMULTPARALLEL as a sub-algorithm to compute A^m for $m \geq 2$.

2 If multiplication requires T_m time units, addition requires T_a time units and, as before, we ignore initializations and overhead, how many time units are required to multiply two $n \times n$ matrices using MATRIXMULTPARALLEL?

3 Modify MATRIXMULTPARALLEL so that it can multiply two matrices A and B, the first of which has dimension $m \times r$ and the second dimension $r \times n$.

4 Now how many time units are required for the matrix multiplication?

Of course, these two examples only scratch the surface of the subject of parallel algorithms. Most serial algorithms don't lend themselves nearly so easily to parallelization as summation and matrix multiplication. In most situations, it is necessary to perform some portion of the computation before other parts can be attempted. However, many computations can be significantly speeded up by taking advantage of whatever inherent parallelism exists in the *problem* to be solved. You may expect the subject of parallel algorithms to grow in importance.

■ ANSWERS TO EXERCISES

Exercise 10.1

1 (a) $b_1 = 19; b_2 = -6; b_3 = 1; sum = 14$; (b) $b_1 = 19; b_2 = 1; b_3 = 4; b_4 = 7; sum = 31$.

2 $2n$ time units for SUMPARALLEL as opposed to $n^2 - 1$ for serial addition.

3 Suppose that the number of items m to be added is such that $(n-1)^2 < m < n^2$. Then just set the values from $m + 1$ to n^2 equal to 0 and use SUMPARALLEL.

4 With the input and output as in SUMPARALLEL, here is the algorithm:

```
for i = m − 1 downto 0
    parallel j = 1 to 2^i
        a_j ← a_{2j−1} + a_{2j}          [Add pairs in parallel]
    endparallel
endfor
```

This algorithm overwrites the original values of a_{ij}. If you don't want to do this, first add pairs of a_{ij}s, putting them into $b_i, i = 1, 2, \ldots, 2^{m-1}$ and then add pairs of the b_is as in the algorithm above.

The number of time units required by this algorithm is just $m = \log_2 n$ which is much better than SUMPARALLEL for large n. Indeed, this algorithm is the best possible unless you have a processor which can simultaneously add more than two numbers at a time.

5 To calculate $h_i, i = 1, \ldots, 2N + 1$, initialize h_1 to 1 and h_2 to 3 and then use:

```
parallel j = 1 to 2
    for i = 1 to N
        h_{2i+j} ← 4h_{2(i−1)+j} + 3
    endfor
endparallel
```

Exercise 10.2

1 Let MatrixMultParallel have three arguments with the
first two representing the two $n \times n$ matrices and the third
giving the location of the result. Then here is an algorithm to
compute A^m.

Input $m, n, a_{ij}, i, j = 1, 2, \ldots, n$

Algorithm MatrixPowerParallel

> MatrixMultParallel(A, A, B) [Compute $B = A^2$]
> **for** $k = 3$ **to** m
> > MatrixMultParallel(A, B, C)
> >
> >   [Compute successive powers of A]
> > $B \leftarrow C$ [A^k replaces A^{k-1}]
> **endfor**

Output C [$= A^m$]

Note that replacing B by C could also be done by a parallel
algorithm.

2 $nT_m + (n - 1)T_a$.

3 **Input** $m, r, n, a_{ik}, i = 1, 2, \ldots, m, k = 1, 2, \ldots, r,$
$\qquad\qquad b_{kj}, k = 1, 2, \ldots, r, j = 1, 2, \ldots n$

Algorithm NonsquareParMult

> **parallel** $i = 1$ **to** m
> > **parallel** $j = 1$ **to** n
> > > $c_{ij} \leftarrow a_{i1}b_{1j}$
> > > **for** $k = 2$ **to** r
> > > > $c_{ij} \leftarrow c_{ij} + a_{ik}b_{kj}$
> > > **endfor**
> > **endparallel**
> **endparallel**

Output C [$= AB$]

4 $rT_m + (r - 1)T_a$.

11
String algorithms

This chapter is, as was a major portion of Chapter 5, concerned with searching. But whereas in Chapter 5 we discussed searching in lists of items, such as a personnel file, this chapter is concerned with searching in *strings* of characters (i.e. any sequence of characters) such as those produced on a word processor. Think how often you use word processor functions such as Find or Replace or Spell Check. Each of these, particularly the latter, requires a rapid search through your document (and, for spell checking, through a dictionary also) to find particular patterns. Computers are so fast today that, since most documents produced on a word processor are relatively short, the speed of the search may not be crucial in the sense that you would notice much if a poor rather than a good search algorithm were used. But consider searching for a subject in a library catalogue or in a large database of documents. In these cases, it is still – and will remain – important to search as efficiently as possible. This chapter is concerned with efficient algorithms to search for patterns (e.g. words) in strings of characters.

First, some notation: denote the string being searched by

$$S = s_1 s_2 \cdots s_n$$

where each s_i is a character from whatever alphabet is appropriate (e.g. letters, letters plus punctuation, digits) and where n may be very large, in the thousands or even millions. Let the pattern we are searching for be denoted by

$$P = p_1 p_2 \cdots p_m$$

where p_i is from the same alphabet as s_i and m is usually not large (say, < 50) and, in any case, is much smaller than n.

1 Brute force search

A *brute force* algorithm, like a greedy algorithm (see Chapter 7), takes the path of least resistance and just ploughs ahead. Greedy algorithms, as in the case of MINSPANTREE, sometimes work and, when they do, are generally good solutions to the problems they are trying to solve. Brute force algorithms, on the other hand, always work but are almost never a good way of approaching a problem because they tend to be very inefficient.

What then would be a brute force approach to finding the first occurrence of P in S? Just try matching P starting at s_1 and, if this doesn't work, try starting at s_2 etc. Algorithm 11.1 implements this idea. When you work through (1) in Exercise 11.1, you will see just how this algorithm works.

Input n, S, m, P [String S and pattern P and their lengths]

Algorithm BRUTESEARCH

    for $i = 1$ **to** $n - m + 1$
                      [$n - m + 1$ last possible match position]
        $j \leftarrow 1$ [Initialization]
        repeat while $j \leq m$ **and** $p_j = s_{i+j-1}$
            $j \leftarrow j + 1$ [Try next character]
        endrepeat
        if $j = m + 1$ **then stop**   [Pattern found]
    endfor   [Failure; try next position]
    print 'failure'   [Overall failure]

Output i [Position of p_1 in S]
    or
    'failure'

Algorithm 11.1: Brute force string search

■ **EXERCISE 11.1**

1 Apply BRUTESEARCH to the following cases (where the spaces are shown only to improve readability).

- $S = rst\ urt\ urs\ trs\ urs\ trs\ trr\ st$
  $P = rst\ rst\ rrs\ t$
- $S = 244\ 152\ 423\ 244\ 512\ 441\ 524\ 21$
  $P = 244\ 152\ 421$
- $S = aaa\ aaa\ aaa\ aaa\ aaa\ aaa\ b$
  $P = aaa\ ab$

In each case count the number of comparisons of one character with another (in the **repeat while** statement) that you make.

2 Explain why s_{i+j-1} is the correct subscript in the **repeat while** statement and why $n - m + 1$ is correct in the **for** statement.

3 Use the result of the third problem in (1) to infer the worst case of the number of comparisons as a function of m and n when P actually can be found in S. Suppose P is not in S. What is the worst case then?

4 Suppose that the alphabet from which S and P are composed has k characters and that each of the k is equally likely in any position of S or P. Then about how many comparisons would you expect to have to make, as a function of m and k, before a first successful match is found? (Assume that n is very large compared to m.) Note that the assumptions in this problem are highly unrealistic because, effectively, we are assuming that both S and P are random strings.

2 Precomputation and string searching

Suppose you're seaching for the pattern 'there' in a string which begins 'The third man thought ...'. When you compare the pattern with the beginning of the string, the match fails at the fourth position (space). But there's no point in now starting at the second position because the match of the two 'h's at that position means that 't' will not match when you slide (in effect) the pattern one space to the right; similarly for the third position. So the success of the matches at positions 2 and 3 mean that you might as well start the next attempt at a match at position 4. The general question is: can you use the information gleaned from an attempt to match P with S starting at position i in S to skip some positions $i+1, i+2, \ldots$ when attempting the next match? That is, can you do better than brute force? The aim of this section is to show that, indeed, you can.

From here on our examples will be of sequences of characters which are not English text, because these make it easier to explain what we are doing and because actual strings S may not be ordinary text, for example when dealing with coded text.

So first: if a match of P against S fails at position i in S, does that mean that we should begin the next attempt at matching at position i (if $s_i = p_1$) or at position $i+1$ (if $s_i \neq p_1$)? No, because suppose

$$
\begin{aligned}
S &= a \quad b \quad a \quad b \quad a \quad d \quad \ldots \\
P &= a \quad b \quad a \quad d.
\end{aligned}
$$

The first failure would be the b in position 4 of S against the d in position 4 of P but, if we started the next search at position 5 of S, we would miss the match at positions 3–6 of S. So things are not quite as simple as we might wish.

How then do we determine where we can start the next search after a failure, in order to do better than brute force? The answer lies in analysing the pattern P. Consider the 10-character pattern $P = wxywxywywx$ and let us ask the question: if the match of this pattern against any S fails at position j of P, where should we start the next search? We reason as follows (assuming for convenience that we are attempting a match starting at s_1):

- If $s_1 \neq w$, then we can do no better than start next at s_2 because the actual pattern might appear in $s_2 \cdots s_{11}$.

- If the first failure is at $s_2 \neq x$, then again we must start at s_2 because s_2 might be w.

- If the first failure is at $s_3 \neq y$, then we may start at s_3 because, since $s_2 = x$, there is no point in starting at s_2 since $p_1 = w \neq x$.

- If the first failure is at $s_4 \neq w$, then we can start at s_5 because we have already discovered that neither s_2 nor s_3 (which equal x and y, respectively) nor s_4 equals w.

Continuing in this way, we may develop the following table where i is the position in S at which a match failed.

j, failure position in P	Place in S to start next match
1	$i + 1$
2	i
3	i
4	$i + 1$
5	i
6	i
7	$i + 1$
8	$i - 4$
9	$i + 1$
10	i

Note, in particular, that failure at position 8 requires the next match to start at position $i - 4$. Why is this (Q1)? Note also that, if $j = 10$, the next starting position in S is $9 \ (= 10 - 1)$ after the previous start. It is important to understand that the table above is independent of S so that, once calculated for any pattern P, it can be used for any S that P is to be matched against. What we need though is an *algorithm* to compute the table above for any P. If you have answered Q1 above, you will see that the key to this is to match P *against itself* to determine how a failure at position j in P (and i in S so that the previous match started at position $i - j + 1$ in S) can be used to determine where in S between $i - j + 2$ and $i + 1$ to start the next match.

When $j = 1$, the next match must start at $i + 1$ (why (Q2)?). The general rule for $j > 1$ follows:

If the failure is at position j, then start the next match at position $i - k, 0 \leq k \leq j - 2$ for the largest value of k such that

$$p_{k+1} \neq p_j \text{ and } p_r = p_{j-k+r-1}, \quad r = k, k-1, \ldots, 1$$

or $i + 1$ if there is no value of k for which these equations are satisfied.

This is quite tricky. It works because, if the given conditions are satisfied for any k, then P *could* match S starting at position $i - k$. The largest possible k gives the earliest position in S where the pattern could match the string. But if the conditions are satisfied for no k, then no match is possible starting at any character already looked at (i.e. up to and including i in S) so you can do no better than start the next match at $i + 1$. Algorithm 11.2 embodies all the thoughts above. The vector *start* gives the position for starting the next match relative to i, the position in S where the previous match failed.

■ EXERCISE 11.2

1 Hand trace NEWSTART for the pattern $P = wxywxywywx$ to obtain the table given above (without the is) for this pattern.

2 What is the array *start* for each of the following patterns?

- *abababcabc*

- *abcdefg*

3 What property must the pattern P of length m have if the next search always starts at position $i+1$ in S when the present search fails at position i?

Now we can use NEWSTART as a subalgorithm in our search algorithm. But note first that, while tricky, NEWSTART has to be executed only once at the beginning of the search after which the values of *start* can be used throughout the search. This idea of *precomputation* before attacking directly the problem you wish to solve is often a powerful technique for increasing efficiency. Algorithm 11.3 searches a string for a pattern using NEWSTART.

This algorithm, known as the Knuth-Morris-Pratt or KMP algorithm, is short and sweet but it has some tricky aspects which the exercise that follows it will elucidate.

Input m, P $\qquad$ [m is the length of P]

Algorithm NewStart

> $start(1) \leftarrow 1$ $\qquad$ [If fail at position 1 in j,
> $\qquad\qquad\qquad\qquad\qquad$ must restart at $i+1$ in P]
> $j \leftarrow 2$ $\qquad\qquad\qquad\qquad$ [Initialization]
> **repeat until** $j > m$
> $\quad$ $k \leftarrow j - 2$ $\qquad$ [Initialization to largest value of k]
> $\quad$ **repeat while** $k \geq 0$
> $\qquad$ $flag \leftarrow 0$ $\qquad\qquad$ [$flag$ set to 1 after failure]
> $\qquad$ **if** $p_j = p_{k+1}$ **then** $flag \leftarrow 1$ $\qquad$ [Failure for this k]
> $\qquad$ **if** $flag = 0$ **then**
> $\qquad\quad$ $r \leftarrow 1$ $\qquad\qquad\qquad\qquad$ [Initialise]
> $\qquad\quad$ **repeat while** $r \leq k$
> $\qquad\qquad$ **if** $p_r \neq p_{j-k+r-1}$ **then**
> $\qquad\qquad\quad$ $flag \leftarrow 1$; **exit** $\qquad$ [Failure for this k]
> $\qquad\qquad$ **endif**
> $\qquad\qquad$ $r \leftarrow r + 1$ $\qquad\qquad\qquad$ [Try next r]
> $\qquad\quad$ **endrepeat**
> $\qquad\quad$ **if** $flag = 0$ **then**
> $\qquad\qquad$ $start(j) \leftarrow -k$; **exit** $\qquad$ [Success]
> $\qquad\quad$ **endif**
> $\qquad\quad$ $k \leftarrow k - 1$ $\qquad\qquad$ [Failure; try next k]
> $\qquad$ **endif**
> $\quad$ **endrepeat**
> $\quad$ **if** $flag = 1$ **then**
> $\qquad$ $start(j) \leftarrow 1$ $\qquad\qquad\qquad$ [Failure for all k]
> $\quad$ **endif**
> $\quad$ $j \leftarrow j + 1$ $\qquad\qquad\qquad\qquad$ [Next j]
> **endrepeat**

Output $start(j), j = 1, 2, \ldots, m$

Algorithm 11.2: Precomputation for string search

Input n, S, m, P [String, pattern and lengths]

Algorithm SMARTSEARCH

    NEWSTART   [Calculate *start* array]
    $i \leftarrow 1; j \leftarrow 1$ [Initialization of pointers to S, P]
    repeat while $i \leq n - m + 1$ [$n - m + 1$ last possible start]
      repeat while $j \leq m$ [Search for match]
        if $s_i = p_j$ **then** $i \leftarrow i + 1; j \leftarrow j + 1$
                else exit   [Match failed]
        endif
      endrepeat
      if $j > m$ **then print** $i - m$; **stop**   [Success]
           else $i \leftarrow i + start(j); j \leftarrow 1$ [Restart values]
      endif
    endrepeat
    print 'failure'   [No match possible]

Output $i - m$ [Position of p_1 in S.]
    or
    'failure'

Algorithm 11.3: String search with precomputation

━━━━━━━━━━━━━━━━━━━━━━━━━━━━━━━━━━━━━━

■ EXERCISE 11.3

1 When a match fails why is the replacement of the current i by $i + start(j)$ the correct new value of i?

2 Apply NEWSTART and then SMARTSEARCH to each of the strings and patterns of (1) in Exercise 11.1 to determine how many comparisons are needed in each case.

We have by no means fully plumbed the depths of the subject of searching for patterns in strings. There are other effective algorithms besides SMARTSEARCH and other improvements which can be made if there is some *a priori* information about the character (pun intended) of S or P. But this chapter should have given you the flavour of this important class of algorithms.

■ ANSWERS TO QUESTIONS

Q1 If the match fails in position 8 (because the character of S is not y), then characters 4–7 (of the portion of S being matched against) must be $wxyw$ and it is possible that P matches S starting at position $i - 4$ (since the first four characters of P are $wxyw$ and the fifth character (x) could match the position that y did not match).

Q2 When the first character of the pattern does not match the string at position i, then it is always possible that, starting at position $i + 1$ in S, P matches S.

■ ANSWERS TO EXERCISES

Exercise 11.1

1 Number of comparisons: 34, 37, 75.

2 $i+j-1$ is the position of the jth character if the first character is in s_i. If you start after s_{n-m+1}, then there won't be m characters to match P against.

3 The worst case occurs when you have to compare each of the m elements of P against characters of S and when success is never achieved until the m characters that start at s_{n-m+1}. So the worst case number of comparisons is $m(n - m + 1)$. The worst case when P does not occur in S is precisely the same. Note that the third problem in (1) is an example of a worst case with $m = 5, n = 19$ and $m(n - m + 1) = 75$.

4 The probability that any match of a character from P with a character from S is successful is $1/k$. So the probability of m consecutive matches and, therefore, a successful search for P, is $(1/k)^m$. Thus, the probable number of positions in S for which you will have to try a match is the reciprocal of this or k^m. But how many comparisons will you have to try, on average, for each starting position in S, except the last, before you fail? This is a difficult computation; the result is

$$\frac{1}{k-1}\left(k - \frac{1}{k^{m-1}}\right).$$

If you multiply this by one less than the probable number of positions (i.e. those at which you fail to find a match) and then add m for the one where you do find a match, you get the average number of comparisons you make in finding the pattern P. Whew! If nothing else, this should convince you that the analysis of algorithms is a difficult subject.

Exercise 11.2

1 We show the trace for $j = 4, 8$ since these two values illustrate all aspects of NEWSTART.

$j = 4$	k	$flag$	r	Comment
	2	0		Possible success since $p_3 \neq p_4$
		0	2	Failure since $p_2 \neq p_3$
		1		
	1	0		Possible success since $p_2 \neq p_4$
		0	1	Failure since $p_1 \neq p_3$
		1		
	0	0		Failure since $p_1 = p_4$
		1		

Since there is failure for all values of k, $start(4) = 1$.

$j = 8$	k	$flag$	r	Comment
	6	0		Possible success since $p_7 \neq p_8$
		0	6	Failure since $p_6 \neq p_7$
		1		
	5	0		Failure since $p_6 = p_8$
		1		
	4	0		Possible success since $p_5 \neq p_8$
		0	4	Possible success since $p_4 = p_7$
		0	3	Possible success since $p_3 = p_6$
		0	2	Possible success since $p_2 = p_5$
		0	1	Success since $p_1 = p_4$

Since all conditions are satisfied, $start(8) = -k = -4$.

2 First pattern: 1 0 1 0 1 0 −4 1 0 −2
Second pattern: 1 0 0 0 0 0

3 All the characters of P must be the same.

Exercise 11.3

1 When a match fails, the current value of i is the position in S where the match failed. Therefore, since $start(j)$ is the position relative to this position in S at which the new match should start (with negative values meaning positions in S before i), $i + start(j)$ is the correct new value of i.

2 First pattern: *start* is 1 0 0 1 0 0 1 -4 0 0; NEWSTART requires 34 comparisons and the rest of SMARTSEARCH requires 19 comparisons for a total of 53. Note, in particular, that *start* differs in only one position from that for the pattern *wxywxywywx*. Do you see why this is so? Second pattern: 1 0 0 0 0 1 0 -2 -1; 26; 21; 47. Third pattern: 1 1 1 1 -3; 6; 61; 67.

12
Verification of algorithms

Algorithmics, as noted in Chapter 1, is about the design, analysis and verification of algorithms. All previous chapters of this book have been about the design of algorithms and we have regularly discussed their analysis when we compared the efficacy of more than one algorithm for the same task and when we explicitly considered how rapidly an algorithm executed its task. In this chapter we shall consider the verification of algorithms, the most difficult aspect of algorithmics and the one, therefore, on which the least progress has been made. Necessarily, we shall only be able to give you the flavour of this aspect of algorithmics with some examples of the verification of algorithms.

1 Verification of the multiplication algorithm

In Chapter 1 we presented Algorithm 1.3 to perform multiplication by repeated addition. Here it is again as Algorithm 12.1 but with some embellishments which we'll discuss below.

We expect that you were able to convince yourself that this algorithm does what it purports to do while reading Chapter 1 or, at least, you can easily do so now after reading the foregoing eleven chapters of this book. But for more complicated algorithms it won't be at all obvious whether they really do what they are supposed to do. So some *formal* technique – which always means

Input x [Integer ≥ 0]

      y [Any integer]

Algorithm MULT

    $\{A_1 : x \geq 0\}$ [Input specification]

    $prod \leftarrow 0; u \leftarrow 0$ [Initialize $prod$ and u]

    $\{A_2 : prod = uy\}$ [Loop invariant]

    repeat until $u = x$ [When $u = x$ skip rest of loop]

        $prod \leftarrow prod + y$

        $u \leftarrow u + 1$

    endrepeat

    $\{A_3 : prod = uy$ **and** $u = x\}$ [Loop termination condition]

    $\{A_4 : prod = xy\}$ [Output specification]

Output $prod$ [$= xy$]

Algorithm 12.1: Multiplication algorithm with assertions

---

a *mathematical* technique – will be needed. Illustrating such a technique on a simple algorithm such as MULT will indicate how it might be used in more complex cases.

The quantities appearing in braces ($\{\dots\}$) in MULT above are called *assertions*. (We have numbered them A_1, A_2, A_3, A_4 so that they can be referred to easily in what follows.) They take the form of *Boolean expressions*, that is expressions which are either true (T) or false (F). Each assertion consists of one or more mathematical expressions, each individually T or F, which, if there is more than one, are connected by **and** or **or**, which have the meanings previously ascribed to them. Additionally, each expression may be preceded by **not** so that if its value is T, it becomes F with **not** before it and vice versa.

These assertions are statements about the state of the variables in an algorithm at a particular place in it. Three types of assertions are particularly noteworthy.

- The *input specification* states the properties which the input variables must satisfy. Thus, $\{x \geq 0\}$ merely repeats the condition stated under **Input**. Since there is no restriction on y, it need not appear in the input specification. (Although you might argue that the input specification should read $\{x, y$ integers, $x \geq 0, -\infty < y < \infty\}$, we believe that, since all our variables are integers, it is unnecessary here to be this explicit and that including the limits on y would just be pedantry.)

- The *output specification* similarly is a statement about the variables at the end of the program. It normally is a statement that the algorithm has computed what it was supposed to compute. Thus $\{prod = xy\}$ asserts that MULT indeed computes the *prod*uct of x and y.

- The *loop invariant* is an assertion about the variables in a **repeat** or **for** loop which is supposed to be true when the loop is first entered and on each subsequent entry into the loop. We'll consider the loop invariant in MULT just below.

To prove an algorithm is correct requires the proof of a sequence of *theorems* involving the assertions and the algorithm itself. For MULT these theorems are:

- $T_1 : A_1 \Rightarrow A_2$. [This should be read: A_1 implies A_2 or, in words, that the truth of the input specification A_1 implies the truth of the loop invariant A_2 before the **repeat** loop is entered the first time.]

- $T_2 : A_2(\text{before}) \Rightarrow A_2(\text{after})$. [That is: does the truth of A_2 at each entry to the loop imply the truth of A_2 when the loop has been executed? Or, in other words: is the loop invariant really invariant? Or, in yet other words: is the loop invariant true on each entry into and, therefore, also on each exit from the loop?]

- $T_3 : A_2 \Rightarrow A_3$. [Or: does the truth of the loop invariant and the fact that the loop has been exited for the last time imply the truth of the *loop termination condition*?]

- $T_4 : A_3 \Rightarrow A_4$. [Does the truth of the loop termination condition imply the truth of the output specification?]

If we can prove each of these theorems, then we will have proved that

$$A_1 \Rightarrow A_4$$

that is, that the truth of the input specification, together with what the algorithm itself does, implies the truth of the output specification.

So can we prove T_1, T_2, T_3 and T_4? Yes, albeit informally, as follows.

T_1: Quite aside from the content of A_1, when A_2 is first reached, *prod* and u are both 0 so *prod* $= uy$ and, hence, A_2 is true.

T_2: If A_2 is true at entry into the loop, that is, if *prod* $= uy$, then in the loop u is increased by 1 and *prod* is increased by y, so *prod* $= uy$ at the end also.

T_3: When the loop terminates, this can only be because $u = x$. Since we know from T_2 that *prod* $= ux$ each time the loop is completed, this means that both expressions in A_3 are true and so A_3 is true.

T_4: But if $u = x$, we may substitute x for u in *prod* $= uy$ to get A_4.

This completes our verification of MULT.

■ **EXERCISE 12.1**

1 y is allowed to be negative or zero in MULT. Is the proof of T_2 valid in these cases? Why?

2 We seem never to have used the input specification in proving $T_1 - T_4$. Does that mean that MULT works even if x is negative? Why?

3 It is not enough to prove that an algorithm does what it is purported to do. You must also show that it *terminates*, that is, that it doesn't, for example, get into an infinite loop. How would you prove that MULT always terminates?

4 Write an algorithm which has as input the real number x and the positive integer n and computes $x + n$ by repeated addition of 1. Insert appropriate assertions in this algorithm and use them to prove that your algorithm is correct and that it terminates.

2 Verification of bubble sort

In Chapter 5 we developed Algorithm 5.3 for bubble sort which we reproduce here as Algorithm 12.2.

Input $n, K_i, i = 1, 2, \ldots, n$

Algorithm BUBBLE

     $i \leftarrow n - 1$ [Position of last comparison]
     repeat
        for $j = 1$ **to** i
           if $K_j > K_{j+1}$ **then** $K_j \leftrightarrow K_{j+1}$ [$\leftrightarrow$ means interchange]
        endfor
        $i \leftarrow i - 1$
     endrepeat when $i = 0$

Output $K_1, K_2, \ldots, K_n$ [In lexical order]

Algorithm 12.2: Bubble sort

Although this algorithm doesn't look much more complex than MULT, it is considerably more difficult to verify. At the least, when we have finished discussing the verification of BUBBLE, you should realize that verifying long, complicated algorithms is very difficult, indeed, in fact, so difficult that it can, as yet, rarely be accomplished.

First, using the terminology developed in the previous section, let's see if we can develop assertions about BUBBLE.

- **Input specification:** This is easy. All we need to be assured of is that the list to be sorted is not empty. So the input specification is: $n > 0$.

- **Output specification:** This is somewhat harder. What

we wish to specify is that, at the end of execution of the algorithm, the list is sorted. One way to do this would be

$$K_1 \leq K_2 \text{ and } K_2 \leq K_3 \text{ and } \ldots \text{ and } K_{n-1} < K_n.$$

This formulation is at best unaesthetic. So, using instead the *universal quantifier* notation from mathematical logic, we may write

$$(\forall j : 1 \leq j \leq n - 1)K_j \leq K_{j+1}$$

which should be read: for all j from 1 to $n - 1$, $K_j \leq K_{j+1}$. You should see that this more compact notation is precisely equivalent to the previous form.

- **Inner loop invariant:** Verification of BUBBLE is harder than verification of MULT mainly because BUBBLE contains two nested loops whereas MULT contains only a single loop. Let us begin with the inner loop (the **for** loop). As j goes from 1 to i, we successively compare adjacent keys and interchange them if the first is greater than the second. So after each pass through the **for** loop, the keys in positions 1 through j are all less than the key in position $j + 1$. Again using quantifier notation, this can be expressed by

$$(\forall r : 1 \leq r \leq j)K_r \leq K_{j+1}.$$

But an immediate problem arises. Is this loop invariant true when the **for** loop is first entered? For how do we know what value j has at this point? The answer is that, by convention, if the first value taken by the **for** loop variable (j) is J, then, implicitly, before entry into the loop, $j = J - 1$. In this case $J = 1$ so the implicit value of j is zero. Is the loop invariant above true when $j = 0$? In this case it becomes

$$(\forall r : 1 \leq r \leq 0)K_r \leq K_1.$$

Is this true? What are the values of r such that $1 \leq r$ and $r \leq 0$? There are none! So the assertion is *empty*. Again by convention, an empty assertion is always true so that our loop invariant is true upon initial entry into the loop. We'll worry later about whether it remains true after each pass through the **for**-loop.

Now how about the loop termination condition for the **for**-loop? Well, it is just that

$$(\forall r : 1 \le r \le i)K_r \le K_{i+1}.$$

Since at the termination of the inner loop $j = i$, the correctness of the loop invariant implies the truth of the loop termination condition.

- **Outer loop invariant:** This is harder. It has three parts:

  1 $0 \le i \le n-1$ which just defines the possible values of i.

  2 $(\forall r : i+2 \le r < n)K_r \le K_{r+1}$ which states that the $n-i-1$ keys at the end have been ordered by previous passes. Note that on first entry into the **repeat** loop, $i = n-1$ so there are no values of r such that $n+1 \le r < n$. Again when $i = n-2$ there are no values of r, which is correct since, after the first pass through the outer loop, only the largest key is in its final resting place in the nth position.

  3 $(\forall r : 1 \le r \le i+1)K_r \le K_{i+2}$ which states that all those keys not yet ordered are less than the key put in its final resting place on the previous pass. Before the first entry into the **repeat** loop, this condition states that all keys are less than or equal to K_{n+1} which is nonexistent but which we define arbitrarily to be ∞.

The entire outer loop invariant is, therefore,

$$(0 \le i \le n-1) \textbf{ and } (\forall r : i+2 \le r < n)K_r \le K_{r+1}$$

$$\textbf{and } (\forall r : 1 \le r \le i+1)K_r \le K_{i+2}.$$

Now all we have to do to complete the verification of BUBBLE is to state and prove the relevant theorems based on the assertions above. Had enough? So have we. All we'll do is draw your attention to some of the aspects of the rest of the verification process in the exercise that follows.

■ EXERCISE 12.2

1 The output specification and the loop termination condition for the outer loop in BUBBLE must be effectively identical. Why?

2 What is the loop termination condition for the outer loop? Show that upon exit from the outer loop, the truth of the outer loop invariant implies the truth of the outer loop termination condition.

3 In the answer to (3) of Exercise 5.3, we described how you could make BUBBLE more efficient by keeping a record during each pass through the inner loop of where the last interchange took place and thereby not doing unnecessary work on the next pass. Modify BUBBLE to implement this idea.

4 How does the modification in (3) change the loop invariants for BUBBLE derived above?

3 Verification of Quicksort

Verification of recursive algorithms is typically quite different from the verification of non-recursive algorithms such as MULT and BUBBLE. We shall illustrate this using QUICKSORT which was developed in Chapter 9 as Algorithm 9.3 and which we reproduce here as Algorithm 12.3 (on page 154).

In order to verify the correctness of QUICKSORT we would have to verify first the correctness of PARTLIST which is, as you will recall, non-recursive. In our discussion here we shall assume that that has already been done and so we know that PARTLIST(s, t) takes the keys from position s to position t and partitions them into two parts separated by the pivot key in position p, such that all items from position s to $p - 1$ are less than or equal to the pivot key and all items from position $p + 1$ to t are greater than or equal to the pivot key.

We are ready then to verify QUICKSORT. Our tool, as in generally the case with recursive algorithms, is mathematical induction.

Input $n, K_i, i = 1, \ldots n$

Algorithm QUICKSORT

procedure QUICK(s, t)	[Recursive procedure]
if $t - s > 0$ **then**	[If $t - s \leq 0$, nothing to sort]
PARTITION(s, t)	[Apply PARTLIST to sublist]
QUICK$(s, p - 1)$	[Recursive call to sort T_1]
QUICK$(p + 1, t)$	[Recursive call to sort T_2]
endif	
return	
endpro	

QUICK$(1, n)$ [Main algorithm call of QUICK]

Output $K_1, K_2, \ldots, K_n$ in sorted order

Algorithm 12.3: Quicksort

The proposition $P(n)$ which we wish to prove is:

$P(n)$: QUICKSORT correctly sorts a list of n items.

The *basis case* $P(1)$ is quickly handled. With the call from the main algorithm being QUICK$(1,1)$, $t - s$ in QUICK is zero so QUICK does nothing, which is the correct action for a list of one element.

Now we apply *strong induction* by assuming that QUICKSORT is correct for all lists of length less than n and then proving that QUICKSORT works for lists of length n. Or, more formally, using the quantifier notation introduced above, we wish to prove that

$$(\forall i : 1 \leq i \leq n - 1)P(i) \Rightarrow P(n).$$

When the length of the list is $n > 1$, the initial call of QUICK from the main algorithm is QUICK$(1, n)$. What happens then? Since $n > 1$, $t - s = n - 1 > 0$ and so PARTLIST(s, t) is called. We have assumed that it correctly performs its task of partitioning the full list into two sublists separated by the pivot key. Note that the length of the longest of these sublists is at most $n - 1$ since the pivot key is not a part of either sublist. So the subsequent calls of QUICK$(1, p - 1)$ and QUICK$(p + 1, n)$ both involve sublists with fewer than n elements. Therefore, by the induction hypothesis that QUICKSORT (and, therefore, QUICK) are correct for lists of length less than n, both QUICK$(1, p - 1)$ and QUICK$(p + 1, n)$ correctly sort their sublists. Because of the property of the pivot key that it is greater than or equal to all keys in the $(1, p - 1)$ list and less than or equal to all keys in the $(p + 1, n)$ list, the result must be a completely sorted list which, as we wished, proves $P(n)$ and, by strong induction, proves that QUICKSORT correctly sorts a list of any length.

You probably found this discussion easier to understand than those about the correctness of either MULT or BUBBLE. This feature of recursive algorithms, namely the fact that their verification can usually be accomplished using mathematical induction, is a particularly attractive advantage of recursion.

■ EXERCISE 12.3

1 We didn't verify PARTLIST but you should be able to state loop invariants for each of the two inner loops in PARTLIST. Try it.
2 Similarly, what is the loop termination condition for the outer loop of PARTLIST?
3 Actually, you have seen a proof or correctness of a recursive algorithm like this before. Where was it?
4 Apply the technique of this section to verify the correctness of DEPTHFIRSTSEARCH in Chapter 7. This is rather more difficult than the verification of QUICKSORT or HANOI.

■ ANSWERS TO EXERCISES

Exercise 12.1

1 Yes, the proof is fine because at no point is it assumed in the proof that $y \geq 0$.
2 No, because as the next part of this exercise considers, proving

correctness is not the same as proving *termination*. Both must be proved in order for the algorithm to work.

3 It terminates because u starts at 0 and increases by 1 at each pass through the loop. Since x is a non-negative integer, sooner or later (if $x = 0$, right at the very beginning), u must equal x at which point the algorithm terminates.

4 Input x, n

Algorithm SUMXN

$$\{A_1 : n > 0\}$$
$$sum \leftarrow x$$
$$\{A_2 : sum = x + i\}$$
$$\textbf{for } i = 1 \textbf{ to } n$$
$$\quad sum \leftarrow sum + 1$$
$$\textbf{endfor}$$
$$\{A_3 : sum = x + i \textbf{ and } i = n\}$$
$$\{A_4 : sum = x + n\}$$

Output *sum*

Here are the theorems we must prove and their proofs.

- $A_1 \Rightarrow A_2$: Since i is implicitly 0 before entry into the loop, this theorem is immediately true.

- A_2(before) $\Rightarrow A_2$(after): Each time through the loop, *sum* and i are both increased by 1 so A_2 is, indeed, a loop invariant.

- $A_2 \Rightarrow A_3$: At exit from the loop, the loop invariant (the first part of A_3) is still true and $i = n$ since this is the condition at the termination of the loop. Therefore, this theorem is also true.

- $A_3 \Rightarrow A_4$: The two clauses in A_3 directly imply the truth of A_4.

The proof that the algorithm terminates is immediate because the **for**-loop always terminates, so that there is no possibility of an infinite loop.

Exercise 12.2

1 Because there are no statements of the algorithm between them.

2 The loop termination condition which, as the previous part of the exercise indicates, is essentially the output condition, namely that the list is now sorted:

$$(\forall j : 1 \leq j \leq n - 1)K_j \leq K_{j+1}$$

.

Since $i = 0$ on exit from the outer loop, the second condition of the loop invariant is:

$$(\forall r : 2 \leq r < n)K_r \leq K_{r+1}$$

and the third part is:

$$(\forall r : 1 \leq r \leq 1)K_r \leq K_2$$

which just says really that $K_1 \leq K_2$. Put this together with the second loop invariant condition just above and you have the output specification.

3 Here is just the algorithm part since the input and output are as in BUBBLE.

```
i ← n - 1
repeat
    t ← 0                    [t = 0 implies no interchange made]
    for j = 1 to i
        if K_j > K_{j+1} then K_j ↔ K_{j+1}          [Interchange]
                              t ← j                   [Set t ≠ 0]
        endif
    endfor
    i ← t - 1        [Place of last interchange for next pass]
endrepeat when t = 0          [End when no interchange]
```

4 The inner loop invariant is unchanged. The outer loop invariant is also unchanged but note that the values of i, instead of being the sequence $n - 1, n - 2, \ldots, 1$, can be any decreasing sequence of non-negative integers starting at $n - 1$.

Exercise 12.3

1 For the first inner loop: $(\forall r : j + 1 \leq r \leq L)K_p \leq K_r$. This just means that the pivot element is less than or equal to all elements from position $j+1$ to position L. Note that, upon first entry into this loop, $j = L$ so that there are no r in the range $j+1 \leq r \leq L$. For the second inner loop: $(\forall r : F \leq r \leq i-1)K_r \leq K_p$. On first entry into this loop, if the pivot is still in position F (i.e. the pivot did not move during the pass through the first inner loop), then this condition just says that $K_F \leq K_F$ which is certainly true.

2 $(\forall r : F \leq r < p)K_r \leq K_p$ **and** $(\forall r : p < r \leq L)K_p \leq K_r$.

3 In the proof of the correctness of HANOI in Chapter 9.

4 Let $P(n)$ be the proposition that: DEPTHFIRSTSEARCH visits all vertices of a connected graph with n vertices.

　　In the basis case for $n = 1$ DEPTH visits the first vertex and marks it visited and then, because $A(u)$ is empty, returns control immediately to the main algorithm and halts.

　　Now suppose that DEPTHFIRSTSEARCH visits all the vertices of any graph with $n - 1$ or fewer vertices and suppose we have a graph with n vertices. Then the call of DEPTH from DEPTHFIRSTSEARCH, after visiting the initial vertex v, chooses a vertex w in $A(v)$, the set of vertices adjacent to v, and calls DEPTH with w as argument. Now w may be considered as the starting vertex of a connected graph with $n - 1$ or fewer vertices (since v, already marked visited, cannot be visited again and 'fewer' because w may not be connected to all the other $n - 1$ vertices of G with, in effect, v deleted from G). By the induction hypothesis (note that this is an application of *strong induction*), DEPTH correctly visits and marks all the vertices of the graph connected to it. When we return to the **for**-loop in DEPTH, there may be no vertices in $A(v)$ still not marked visited, in which case all vertices have been visited and we are finished, or there may be other unvisited vertices in $A(v)$ in which case each is connected to a subgraph of fewer than $n - 1$ vertices and, as above, by the induction hypothesis each vertex of the subgraph is visited. In this way all the vertices are visited [since each vertex of $G - \{v\}$ must be connected to some vertex in $A(v)$] which completes our strong induction proof.

13

Algorithms to computer and calculator programs

Algorithms are interesting mathematical objects on their own. They can be used to develop mathematical theories about the difficulty of solving problems and to compare different techniques for solving the same problem. But if it were not for the fact that algorithms are the basis for most computer programs and that, indeed, algorithms can be converted to computer programs and executed, the subject of algorithms would be of far less importance than it is. In this chapter we shall discuss various aspects of the conversion of algorithms to programs for both computers and programmable calculators so that you can more easily execute the algorithms in this book – as well as others – on your computer or calculator.

1 Algorithms to computer programs

We shall use Pascal as the programming language in which to convert algorithms because it and its variants are widely used. Therefore, the programs we present should be readily understandable. Where our algorithms employ only AL – and no discursive English – their conversion to Pascal is usually straightforward. For example, consider PRIMENUM from Chapter 3. Program 13.1 (overleaf) is a Pascal program which implements this algorithm.

As a second example, Program 13.2 (on page 161) is a Pascal program which implements BISECTION from Chapter 4. It assumes the existence of a function subprogram which computes $f(x)$.

```pascal
program PrimeNum;

var
    i, j, n, m: integer;
    p: array[1..100] of integer;
    k: real;

begin
    readln(m);
    p[1] := 2;
    writeln(p[1]);
    n := 2;
    i := 3;
    repeat
        j := 3;
        repeat
            k := i / j;
            j := j + 2;
        until (j = i) or (trunc(k) * (j - 2) = i);
        if j = i then
            begin
                p[n] := i;
                writeln(p[n]);
                n := n + 1;
            end;
        i := i + 2;
    until n > m;
end.
```

Program 13.1: Prime number program

Both of these examples show a straightforward translation from algorithm to program. So, too, does our third example, Program 13.3 (on page 162), which translates the recursive algorithm HANOI from Chapter 9 to Pascal.

---

program Bisection;

var
    a, b, c, d: integer;
    x: real;
    right, left: real;
    eps: real;
    root: real;

begin
    readln(a, b);
    readln(eps);
    left := a;
    right := r;
    while (right − left) > eps **do**
        begin
            x := (left + right) / 2;
            if f(x) = 0 **then**
              root := x
                    else if f(x) ∗ f(left) < 0 **then**
                      right := x
                            else
                    left := x;
        end;
    root := (left + right) / 2;
    writeln(root);
end.

Program 13.2: Bisection program

Finally in this section, we consider the translation of DEPTHFIRST-SEARCH from Chapter 7 to Pascal. This is not so straightforward because DEPTHFIRSTSEARCH contains some English statements which must be converted somehow into Pascal. The annotations in Program 13.4 (on page 163) will show you how we have done this. Remember, when an algorithm contains statements in English instead of in AL, then this may make the algorithm more readable but it will always make the translation to a program more difficult.

```
program Hanoi;

var
    num, Pinit, Pfin: integer;
    n, r, s: integer;

procedure H(n, r, s: integer);
    begin
        if n =1 then
            writeln('Move ring from Pole ', r, 'to ', s)
                else
            begin
                H(n − 1, r, 6 − r − s);
                writeln('Move ring from Pole ', r, ' to ', s);
                H(n − 1, 6 − r − s, s);
            end;
    end;

begin
        read(num, Pinit, Pfin);
        writeln(num, Pinit, Pfin);
        H(num, Pinit, Pfin);
end.
```

Program 13.3: Towers of Hanoi program

■ **EXERCISE 13.1**

1 Write a Pascal program (or one in any other language you know) to implement PERMUTE in Chapter 4. You will, of course, need

a random number generator to do this but any language you know will have one available.

2 Write a program to implement PARTITIONS from Chapter 3 and use it to find the partitions of $n = 9$ and $n = 10$.

```
program DFS;

var
    a: array[1..n, 1..n] of integer;        (*Adjacency matrix*)
    i, j: integer;
    vis: array[1..n] of integer;  (*For recording visited status*)
    v: integer;

procedure Depth (u: integer);
var
    k, l: integer;
begin
    Visit(u);                    (*A procedure which 'visits' u*)
    vis[u] := 1;                          (*Marks u as visited*)
    writeln(u);           (*Vertices output in order visited*)
    for k := 1 to n do
        begin
            if (u <> k) and (a[u, k] = 1) and (vis[k] = 0)
                then Depth(k);
        end;
end

begin
    readln(n);
    for i := 1 to n do
        for j := 1 to n do
            read(a[i, j]);              (*Input adjacency matrix*)
    for j := 1 to n do
        vis[j] := 0;        (*Mark all vertices 'not visited'*)
    read(v);                                   (*Initial vertex*)
    Depth(v);
end.
```

Program 13.4: Depth first search program

2 *Algorithms to calculator programs*

It will soon be difficult to make a definitive distinction between a calculator and a computer but, for the moment, even calculators which allow programming have rather rudimentary programming languages. We expect that many readers of this book will have programmable calculators and so in this section we shall convert two of our algorithms to a calculator programming language. Our choice of language is that used on the Texas Instruments TI-82, TI-83 and TI-85 calculators.

You may find it instructive to compare Program 13.5 below for PRIMENUM with the Pascal program in the previous section. We have indented this and the calculator program for the Towers of Hanoi to make them easier to read although normally on a calculator you would not use indenting.

```
PrimeNum
Input N
N→dimL1                          [Number of primes to compute]
2→L1(1)                            [List L1 holds primes]
2→M
3→I                              [I is test value for next prime]
Repeat M>N
   1→J
   Repeat J=I or int(I/J)*J=I
      J+2→J                       [Next number to test]
   End
   If I=J                          [If I=J prime found]
        Then
             I→L1(M)
             M+1→M
   End
   I+2→I                          [Next integer to be tested]
End
Disp L1
```

Program 13.5: Calculator program for prime numbers

Users of programmable calculators are sometimes surprised to discover that they can handle recursion quite nicely, although the fact that their procedures cannot have arguments does complicate things a bit. Program 13.6 is a calculator program to implement HANOI. The subprogram H is written below HANOI.

```
Hanoi
Input N
Input R
Input S
H                                        [Call program H]

H                              [Definition of subprogram H]
If N=1
    Then
        Disp R
        Disp S
        Pause
    Else
        N−1→N
        6−R−S→S                          [Pole to move to]
        H                              [Recursive call to H]
        N+1→N                                 [Restore N]
        6−R−S→S                               [Restore S]
        Disp R
        Disp S
        Pause
        N−1→N
        6−R−S→R                        [Pole to move from]
        H                          [Second recursive call]
        N+1→N                                 [Restore N]
        6−R−S→R                               [Restore R]
End
```

Program 13.6: Calculator program for Towers of Hanoi

■ EXERCISE 13.2

1 Write a calculator program to implement FIBONACCI and use it to compute the first 15 Fibonacci numbers.

In this chapter we have only discussed briefly how to convert algorithms to programs. But we hope to have convinced you that, especially when AL rather than English is used in expressing algorithms, the translation of an algorithm to a program, whether for a computer or a calculator, is reasonably straightforward.

■ ANSWERS TO EXERCISES

Exercise 13.1

1 In this Pascal program we use the same function RAND(1, n) that we used in PERMUTE to generate a random integer in the set $\{1, 2, \ldots, n\}$. Different implementations of Pascal will generally have different random number generators available. To run the program below you would have to adapt the random number generator at your installation so that you obtain random integers in the set $\{1, 2, \ldots, n\}$.

```
program Permute;

var
    Flag: array[1..n] of integer;
    i: integer;
    r: integer;
    Perm: array[1..n] of integer;

begin
    readln(n);
    for i := 1 to n do
        Flag[i] := 0;
    for i := 1 to n do
        begin
            repeat
                r := RAND(1,n)
```

```
                until Flag[r] = 0;
                Perm[i] := r;
                Flag[r] := 1
            end;
        for i := 1 to n do
            write(Perm[i]);
        end;
    end.
```

2   **program** Partitions;

var
```
    n, k, m, i, j, c, r, q, h: integer;
    p: array[1..100] of integer;
                    (*To allow partitions of length 100(!)*)
```

begin
```
    readln(n);
    p[1] := n;
    k := 1;
    repeat
        writeln;
        for m := 1 to k do
            write(p[m]);
        if p[k] <> 1 then
            begin
                p[k] := p[k] − 1;
                p[k + 1] := 1;
                k := k + 1;
            end
                    else
            begin
                c := 0;
                i := k;
                while p[i] = 1 do
                    begin
                        c := c + 1;
                        i := i − 1;
                    end;
```

```
            p[i] := p[i] − 1;
            q := trunc((c + 1) / p[i]);
            r := c + 1 − q * p[i];
            j := 1;
            while j <= q do
                begin
                    p[i + 1] := p[i];
                    i := i + 1;
                    j := j + 1;
                end;
            if r = 0 then
                k := i
                    else
                begin
                    k := i + 1;
                    p[k] := r;
                end;
        end;
    until p[1] = 1;
end.
```

Here are the first few partitions of 9:

```
9
8   1
7   2
7   1   1
6   3
6   2   1
6   1   1   1
5   4
```

Exercise 13.2

1   Fibonacci
        15→dimL1   [List L1 stores Fibonacci numbers]
        1→L1(1)
        1→L1(2)
        For (I,3,15)

    L1(I−2)+L1(I−1)→L1(I)
End
Display L1

The first 15 Fibonacci numbers are: 1, 1, 2, 3, 5, 8, 13, 21, 34, 55, 89, 144, 233, 377, 610.

Appendix 1

Summary of algorithmic language

This Appendix summarizes for reference purposes all of the Algorithmic Language (AL) presented in this book. For each part of the language we present, first, its *syntax* (i.e. structure) and then its *semantics* (i.e. its meaning). We will use the following abbreviations: *var* for variable name, *exp* for expression, *int* for integer, *bool* for a Boolean expression. Square brackets ([...]) indicate that the quantity in brackets is optional. Page numbers in parentheses indicate the page on which each structure is first discussed.

Syntax	**Semantics**

Assignment (p. 23):

$$var \leftarrow expression$$

Value of expression replaces value of variable.

Decision (p. 18):

    if *bool* **then**...
        else...
  endif

If *bool* true, do statements after **then**; if false, do statements after **else**.

Iteration:

(p. 15)	**repeat until** *bool* . . . **endrepeat**	Do statements between **repeat** and **endrepeat** while *bool* is false; condition tested at beginning of loop.
(p. 15)	**repeat while** *bool* . . . **endrepeat**	Do statements between **repeat** and **endrepeat** while *bool* is true; condition tested at beginning of loop.
(p. 27)	**repeat** . . . **endrepeat when** *bool*	Do statements between **repeat** and **endrepeat** until *bool* is true; condition tested at end of loop.
(p. 15)	**for** *var* = *int*1 **to** *int*2 [**step** *int*3] . . . **endfor**	Do statements between **for** and **endfor** for each value of *var* from *int*1 to no greater than *int*2 stepping by *int*3. (If *int*3 absent, step by 1.) Or **to** can be replaced by **downto** in which case step is −1 or (negative) *int*3 after **step**.

Loop termination (p. 23):

exit	In a **repeat** or **for** loop ends inner loop; transfer control after **end** of inner loop in which **exit** appears.

Parallel (p. 129):

parallel *var* = *int*1 **to** *int*2 . . . **endparallel**	Execute statements between **parallel** and **endparallel** simultaneously for each value of *var* from *int*1 to *int*2.

Subalgorithms:

(p. 45)	**function** *name* . . . **endfunc**	End execution with **return** between **function** and **endfunc**; function name must appear on left side of assignment.
(p. 92)	**procedure** *name* . . . **endpro**	End execution with **return** between **procedure** and **endpro**; there may be a list of quantities to be returned after **return**.

Input (p. 22):

Input *varlist*	List of variables separated by commas.

Output:

(p. 22)	**Output** *Description*	Description of output.
(pp. 22,30)	**print** *list*	List of literals (set off by '...') and variables separated by commas.

Termination (p. 60):

stop Ends execution

Comment (p. 22):

Anything right
justified in brackets.

Appendix 2

Summary of mathematical notation

This appendix lists all the mathematical notation used in this book which might be unfamiliar to some readers. For each bit of notation we give the symbol and its meaning.

Name	Notation	Meaning
Absolute value function	$\lvert \ldots \rvert$	Value of quantity between vertical bars when that is positive, or negative of that quantity when it is negative.
Approximately equal to	$\approx$	Quantity on the left is approximated by quantity on the right.
Ceiling function	$\lceil \ldots \rceil$	Evaluate the quantity between the $\lceil$ and $\rceil$ and set it equal to the smallest integer greater than or equal to this quantity. Thus, $\lceil 5.2 \rceil = 6$ and $\lceil -3.64 \rceil = -3$.
Ellipsis	$\ldots$ or $\cdots$	Fill in from the quantity to the left of the dots to the quantity to the right of the dots with the implied sequence of omitted quantities. Thus $a_1 + a_2 + \cdots + a_6 = a_1 + a_2 + a_3 + a_4 + a_5 + a_6$.
Empty Set	$\emptyset$	The set with no elements.

Floor function	$\lfloor \ldots \rfloor$	Evaluate the quantity between the $\lfloor$ and $\rfloor$ and set it equal to the largest integer less than or equal to this quantity. Thus, $\lfloor 3.7 \rfloor = 3$ and $\lfloor -5.27 \rfloor = -6$.
Greatest common divisor	$\gcd(m, n)$	The largest positive integer which divides both m and n without remainder; 0 if either m or n is 0.
Implies	$\Rightarrow$	Used to indicate that truth of *proposition* on the left implies truth of proposition on the right.
Integral	$\int$	Represents the integral in calculus.
Interchange	$a \leftrightarrow b$	Replace the value of a with the value of b and vice versa.
Least common multiple	$\text{lcm}(m, n)$	The smallest positive integer which is an integer multiple of both m and n.
Multiplication	$*$	Designates the product of two scalar quantities.
Order	O	$a_n = O(b_n)$ means that, as n gets large (i.e. approaches ∞), the ratio a_n/b_n approaches a constant. That is, the sequence of values a_n *acts like* the sequence b_n.
Summation	$\sum$	$\sum_{i=1}^{n} a_i = a_1 + a_2 + \cdots + a_n$
Universal quantifier	$\forall$	$(\forall j : 1 \leq j \leq n)C_j$ is true if and only if all the conditions C_j, $j = 1, 2, \ldots, n$ are true.

Appendix 3

List of algorithms

Glossary

(Words in definitions in **bold** text are defined elsewhere in the Glossary.)

Assertion   A **statement** inserted in an algorithm (or program) which is used to prove the correctness of an algorithm. It consists of a **Boolean expression** in the variables of the algorithm (e.g. $prod = uy$) which must always be true if the algorithm does what it purports to do.

Assignment statement   The basic computational **statement** in an algorithm. It has the form

$$variable \leftarrow expression$$

and causes the variable to be *assigned* the value of the expression when all of the variables in the expression are given their current values.

Backtracking   An algorithmic method in which a solution is pursued by making a (usually arbitrary) choice whenever more than one possible next step is available. In this way either a solution is found or a dead end is reached at which point you *backtrack* (i.e. retrace your steps) until a point is reached at which a choice not previously taken is available. In this way all possible paths to a solution can be investigated and no path will ever be considered more than once.

Boolean expression   A mathematical expression which consists of variables [which can have the values T(rue) or F(alse)], constants (only T and F are possible) and *logical connectives* (**and, or** and **not**, among others). The value of the Boolean expression is either T or F.

Complex number   A number of the form $a + bi$ where a and b are real numbers and i represents $\sqrt{-1}$.

Complexity   The complexity of an algorithm is concerned with the resources required to execute that algorithm. When, as always in this book, we are concerned with how long it takes to execute an algorithm, we speak of *time complexity* and usually, as we have here, express this in the form $O(n^r)$ where n is the crucial **parameter** of the algorithm and the larger r is, the more slowly the algorithm executes. Sometimes the crucial resource is computer memory in which case we speak of *space complexity*. Finally, the complexity of a particular problem is concerned with the best algorithm possible (or, perhaps, known) for solving that problem. Thus, when time is the resource focused upon, we wish to know how small r above can be in the best algorithm imaginable.

Control variable   A control variable (such as i in INSERTION) in a loop (such as **repeat ... endrepeat**) is the variable which is tested at the beginning or the end of the loop to see whether or not to continue execution of the loop.

Divide-and-conquer algorithm   An algorithm of this type, such as BINSEARCH or QUICKSORT, proceeds by taking the given problem and successively reducing it to smaller and smaller instances of the same problem. Often the reductions involve successive halvings of the original problem.

Flowchart   A flowchart is a pictorial representation of an algorithm in which different algorithmic constructs are represented by different shaped boxes (rectangles for assignment, diamonds for decisions etc.) and arrows show the flow of control from one part of the algorithm to the next.

Greedy algorithm   When an algorithm faces a decision on what to do next and makes that decision on the basis of what is easiest or requires the least effort, it is called greedy. Sometimes, as with MINSPANTREE, the greedy approach leads to efficient algorithms but more often this approach leads to inefficient algorithms or does not work at all.

Inner product In vector algebra an inner product, sometimes called a *dot product*, is the sum of the term by term multiplication of the components of two vectors:

$$\mathbf{x} \cdot \mathbf{y} = (x_1, x_2, \ldots, x_n) \cdot (y_1, y_2, \ldots, y_n) = \sum_{i=1}^{n} x_i y_i$$

Lexical Means, literally, 'pertaining to the words of a language as in a dictionary' so that lexical or *lexicographic* ordering means, for words, alphabetically ordered as in a dictionary but, as appropriate, can also mean a numerical or any other systematic ordering such as that defined for partitions in Chapter 3.

Literal In a programming language or in algorithmic notation, a literal is anything that stands for itself and has, therefore, no **syntactic** or **semantic** significance. Typically, a literal is a quantity or word (e.g. 'failure') in an output (e.g. **print**) statement which is to be output as it appears in the **statement**.

Loop invariant This is a **Boolean expression**, whose variables are those used in a loop in an algorithm, which is supposed to be true when the loop is initially entered and at each subsequent entry into the loop. It should express a relationship among the loop variables which embodies the essence of what the execution of the loop is supposed to accomplish.

Mathematical induction This is a method used to prove the truth of an (often infinite) set of propositions $P(n), n = n_0,$ $n_0 + 1, n_0 + 2, \ldots$ where n_0 is usually 1, by first proving $P(n_0)$ (the *basis case*) and then proving that the truth of $P(n)$ for any n implies the truth of $P(n + 1)$ (the *inductive step*). (*See also* **Strong induction**.)

Overhead This is the time a computer system spends doing things (such as finding where a variable is stored in memory or testing the sign of a variable) which do not contribute directly to the progress of the computation being performed.

Parameter   In an algorithm a parameter is typically a characteristic quantity of a **procedure** or function which determines some important property of the algorithm such as how fast it executes. More generally, in mathematics a parameter is a constant or variable in a function which determines some of its characteristic properties.

Procedure   In an algorithm a procedure is a portion of the algorithm which performs some specific task or function. It may be embedded in the main algorithm itself (such as a procedure to determine if an integer is odd or even) or it may be a separate *subalgorithm* of the main algorithm.

Quantifier   A quantifier in mathematical logic is an operator which makes it possible to make statements about many propositions (i.e. statements claiming that something is true; propositions often take the form of **Boolean expressions**) in a compact notation. Thus, the *universal quantifier* $\forall$ in the form $\forall n\, P_n$ states that this expression is true if and only if the proposition P_n is true for all n. Similarly, the *existential quantifier* $\exists$ in the form $\exists n\, P_n$ states that this expression is true if and only if there is at least one n for which $P(n)$ is true. In using **mathematical induction** we try to prove the truth of $\forall n \geq n_0\, P(n)$.

Recursive paradigm   This is a method of problem solving in which, in effect, you jump into the middle of a problem, assuming that you know how to solve it, and then work your way out by successively reducing the problem you wish to solve to 'smaller' versions of the problem (typically versions with a **parameter** that is smaller than that for the problem you wish to solve) until you arrive at so simple a version of the problem that you really do know how to solve it. Applying the recursive paradigm leads, therefore, to recursive algorithms. The recursive paradigm is often contrasted to the *inductive paradigm* in which you first compute some values for small versions of the characteristic **parameter**, then infer the general solution from these and, finally, prove (usually by **mathematical induction**) that your solution is correct. This approach usually leads to iterative algorithms.

Roundoff   Roundoff or *rounding error* can result when an arithmetic operation is performed on two numbers in a computer and the result has more digits than can be accommodated in the memory of the computer. Although the resulting error is small in each case, the accumulation of these errors after thousands or even millions of calculations can cause final results to be seriously in error unless careful precautions are taken.

Semantics   In linguistics this refers to the meaning of words, phrases and sentences. In algorithmic language or a programming language it refers to the meaning (as opposed to the structure) of the constructs of the language. (Compare with **Syntax**.)

Statement   A statement in algorithmic language or a programming language is the basic construct out of which algorithms or programs are built. Thus, we have **assignment statements**, *decision* statements, *loop* control statements etc.

Strong induction   In this variant of the usual situation with **mathematical induction**, the proposition $P(n + 1)$ is proved using any or all of the propositions $P(n_0), P(n_0 + 1), \ldots, P(n)$.

Syntax   In language this refers to the correct (or *grammatical*) construction of sentences. In our algorithmic language or a programming language, it refers to the correct construction of the **statements** of the language. (Compare with **Semantics**.)

Bibliography

There are many books which treat the subject of algorithms generally or specific aspects of the subject. The books listed here are a small sampling of the literature on algorithms for those who would like to explore this subject further.

Brassard, G. and Bratley, P. [1988]: *Algorithmics: Theory and Practice*, Englewood Cliffs, NJ: Prentice Hall. [Focuses on the design and analysis of algorithms; intended for advanced undergraduates or beginning post-graduates.]

Horowitz, E. and Sahni, S. [1978]: *Fundamentals of Computer Algorithms*, Potomac, MD: Computer Science Press. [A readable introduction to the design and analysis of algorithms; discusses and presents programs for many of the algorithms in this book.]

Knuth, D. E. [1973, 1981, 1973]: *The Art of Computer Programming*, Vol. 1 (second edition), Vol. 2 (second edition), Vol. 3, Reading, MA: Addison-Wesley. [A classic about algorithms and their analysis, packed with information but not easy to read, particularly for those without a good mathematics background.]

Parberry, I. [1995]: *Problems on Algorithms*, Englewood Cliffs, NJ: Prentice Hall. [Over 650 problems – generally more difficult than the exercises in this book – about and related to algorithms including many in this book.]

Sedgwick, R. [1983]: *Algorithms*, Reading, MA: Addison-Wesley. [Another classic which covers many of the algorithms in this book; lots of Pascal programs but explanations are rather terse.]

Index

(Glossary entries are in italics; a page number in italics represents the main reference for that item.)